# JOSEPH'S WAY

## THE CALL TO FATHERLY GREATNESS

# PRAYER OF FAITH

## 80 DAYS TO UNLOCKING YOUR POWER AS A FATHER

### DEVIN SCHADT

EDITED BY L. JOSEPH HEBERT JR.

Distributed by Ignatius Press

Printed in the United States of America
ISBN: 978-0-9899242-0-7

*To God the Father,*
*from Whom all fatherhood on earth*
*receives its name.*
*May the fatherhood*
*of every man*
*flourish to the praise and the glory*
*of Your Name.*

# Contents

## PRAYER OF HOPE

*Introduction*

# DAY 1

My dear brother in Christ, ours is an age in which mankind has been given profound gifts in the realm of intellect, power, and design: the ability to master the elements of the world, to create what once seemed impossible, to make discoveries unthinkable to previous generations. Humanity, using these great gifts, has made substantial technological advances that have shaped and influenced our lives to no small degree. Many of these advances are good in themselves and assist men in leading adaptive, efficient, prosperous, and comfortable lives. Often however, in receiving such tremendous powers, man has come to believe that his successes and glories are due to his genius alone. In consequence, the creature neglects the Creator, forgetting that the gift has a Giver, forgetting that what humanity has received has been granted by divine providence.

The diminishment, neglect, disrespect, and, in some cases, abhorrence of fatherhood encountered in our outwardly prosperous society is intimately connected to our alienation from and neglect of God. As in the technological realm, so too in the realm of morality, modern man, impressed with his own ability to solve problems, often seeks progress without consulting God or obeying the order of creation. This type of problem solving without the Creator creates a multitude of problems.

For example, modern man's desire to be inclusive of all religions often renders him incapable of taking seriously any religion at all. So too, the promotion of female rights has frequently led not only to the diminishment of the rights of men, but also to a reduction of

woman herself, pressuring her to assume a pseudo-masculine character rather than experiencing the glory and dignity of her feminine
genius. This dynamic can be seen within the Church, where many
have felt pressured to alter the faith in order to make worship more
appealing to the feminine sex. Some have even preached a feminine
Gospel, promising women the possibility of performing functions
which Christ ordained for men, crafting more feminine messages,
and softening the tones of the Sacred Liturgy, implying all the while
that the Church is now ashamed of men.

This dynamic, to a great degree, has feminized men, making
them believe that their masculinity should be shrouded or masked
and most certainly never imposed upon the world. This reduction of the masculine character of men has had catastrophic consequences for the family and the Church. In fact, the number of
men active in the Church today is significantly less than that of
women. Among the fruits of this demographic shift are a radical
decline in vocations to the priesthood and religious life, a decline
in fathers attending Mass, and a consequent decline in biological
fathers embracing their sacred vocation as fathers. As a result, the
fundamental cell of society, the family, is now struggling to be what
it is, divided and uncertain of its purpose, of its importance, and of
the reason God created it.

Much of this confusion in the Church and in the home is due
to men and women, husbands and wives, losing touch with their
sexual genius and their sexual identity, and hence losing sight of the
meaning of who they really are. Man images God not so much in
his solitude as in his communion with the opposite sex.[1] Husband
and wife, by means of their complimentary natures, are capable
of entering into a union that images the Triune God while also
transmitting something of God's divine love to humanity. This pre-

[1]    John Paul II, *Theology of the Body*, *Man Becomes the Image of God* by
Communion of Persons, General audience of Wednesday, 14 November
1979

supposes that the man and the woman first individually become who they are created to be, fulfilling their sexual genius as male and female. If male and female do not fulfill their sexual nature by allowing God to bring their particular sexual genius to full stature through the process of redemption, but rather allow themselves to become feminized men or masculinized women, they lose their self-knowledge and become incapable of giving themselves to one another. In turn, a person who cannot give himself away will fail to arrive at a deeper knowledge of himself or of his God.

By means of their sexual complementarity, true women assist men in becoming real men, and true men assist women in becoming real women. Our sexual identity crisis, by diminishing the power of the father to live and lead his family to live in accordance with the Gospel, has debilitated the Church as a whole in its mission to proclaim the Gospel to a fallen world.

The shadow of sin and the fall of man began with the absent, silent Adam failing to assume his vocational duty to defend his bride against Satan, allowing the infection of sin and death to be transmitted to the entire human family. So also today, man, as defender of the bride and family, is faltering in his defense of children, life, woman, fruitfulness, and even in defense of himself, his vocational role, his duties and responsibilities as husband and father. In other words, many men are losing the battle to become men, and many fathers are not fathering.

My brother, as the identity of the human father diminishes, the recognition of God as Father diminishes in the soul of mankind. Humanity, in attempting to exalt those women formerly belittled, has often belittled those men formerly exalted, and in doing so, has obscured the beauty of the profound union between man and woman—a union God created to signify the great mystery of Christ and His Church, and even the communion of Persons of the Triune Godhead. By denying the fatherhood of man, man denies the Fatherhood of God. This divine Fatherhood is the core of the incarnate Word's Gospel: God is Father. Indeed, Christ made known the God Who is the benevolent, merciful, loving, all-powerful Father, Who is becoming tragically more and more unknown to man today. By losing knowledge of our human fatherhood, we grow more distant from God the Father, distanced from our vocation, our wives, our children and our own identity; and so the family, the micro-church, weakens and diminishes, thereby weakening the macro-Church, the great family of God, itself comprised of families.

If the macro-Church is to be revitalized and strengthened, the micro-church of the family must be restored, strengthened, and given a new vitality. If families are to experience renewal, fathers must fulfill their vocational call from God to become icons of the Heavenly Father. Even while the clouds of despair loom overhead, we cannot allow any excuse to cause us to lose hope. Fatherhood is being restored.

This letter to you, my brother, speaks of the hope of the restoration of fatherhood, which will help restore the family, and which will consequently aid in the restoration of the Church. This letter of fatherly encouragement is intended to edify you and, at times, admonish you, in hopes of inspiring you, by God's grace, to become the father you are called to be by God the Father. This letter, then, concerns the identity of God as Father, the fatherhood of the patriarchs, the fatherhood of St. Joseph, and also your fatherhood viewed in light of these. As you read this letter prayerfully, you will indeed encounter God the Father, the patriarchal fathers, St. Joseph the father of the Son of God, and also, God willing, yourself—as the father you are, and as the father you are called to be.

# DAY 2

## The Allegory of Fatherhood

St. Thomas Aquinas maintained that sacred Scripture can be interpreted in two ways: literally, that is, historically; and symbolically, that is, spiritually. The spiritual sense has a three-fold division: the allegorical sense, the moral sense, and the anagogical sense.

> For as the Apostle says (Hebrews 10:1) the Old Law is a figure of the New Law, and Dionysius says (Coel. Hier. i) 'the New Law itself is a figure of future glory.' Again, in the New Law, whatever our Head has done is a type of what we ought to do. Therefore, so far as the things of the Old Law signify the things of the New Law, there is the allegorical sense; so far as the things done in Christ, or so far as the things which signify Christ, are types of what we ought to do, there is the moral sense. But so far as they signify what relates to eternal glory, there is the anagogical sense.[2]

The "Old Law" is the Old Testament; the "New Law" is the New Testament; our "future glory" is Heaven. The allegorical sense, based on the literal sense, signifies a deeper, symbolic, spiritual meaning, usually revealing something new by describing something old. This sense is therefore a hinge opening up the Old Testament Scriptures to teach us how we are to live under the New, and to what we should look forward in hope. For example, Moses (symbolic of Christ) leads the Hebrews (symbolic of the Church, Christ's body) through the exodus (symbolic of salvation), from

---

[2]     Thomas Aquinas, *Summa Theologica* I 1,10

slavery (symbolic of sin) to Pharaoh (symbolic of Satan), ruler of Egypt (symbolic of a fallen world), across the Red Sea (symbolic of death), through the wilderness (symbolic of Purgatory), to the Promised Land (symbolic of Heaven).[3]

Like the Old Testament, human fatherhood can be viewed as both literal and allegorical; as both historically real, and symbolic; as standing in need of God's direction, yet capable of directing humanity to true Fatherhood, God's Fatherhood. Though God's Fatherhood existed prior to human fatherhood, human fatherhood is not the fulfillment of a type, as though God is the sign of man; for God is not symbolic, but rather most real. Human fatherhood, though real, is more symbolic than real; more like a sign directing humanity toward the Fulfillment or reality of fatherhood, which is God the Father. Recalling the words of St. Paul, "For this reason I bend my knees to the Father of our Lord Jesus Christ from Whom all fatherhood in heaven and on earth receives its name,"[4] we understand that human fatherhood has received its name, its identity, from God the Father, Who truly is Father. "In no way is God in man's image,"[5] but rather man is made in God's image.

Human fatherhood was created and instituted by God to symbolize the divine fatherhood and direct humanity to it. Human fatherhood, having its share of failings, mistakes, fallen tendencies, and sins, appears to offer ample excuse for humanity to disbelieve the proposal of its iconic value. Despite this problem, however, the frequent ability of imperfect, fallen men to love and desire good for their children powerfully signifies the glory and perfection of the all-benevolent, perfectly loving, and completely merciful Father.

Speaking of the Father's generosity in comparison to human fatherhood, Our Lord said, "Therefore, if you who are evil as you

---

3    Peter Kreeft, *A Shorter Summa Pg 43, footnote 11*

4    Ephesians 3:15

5    CCC 370.

are, know how to give good gifts to your children, how much more will your Father in heaven give good things to those who ask Him."[6] Thus human fatherhood has been created by God to lead the creature to the Creator by means of either a negative or positive association. As we will see, the negative and positive aspects of human fatherhood will provide a springboard for our reflection upon the divine Fatherhood. In order to profit from the typology of both human fatherhood and the Old Testament, the focus of this letter will be upon the patriarchs of old: those earthly father-rulers, who by means of both negative and positive example, grant insight into God's Fatherhood. In order to obtain the deepest understanding of the connection between their human fatherhood and the divine Fatherhood, we will study the patriarchs' example through the lens of St. Joseph's new and inspiring fatherhood.

The truths of the Old Testament patriarchs are a type, a foreshadowing, of the new patriarch Joseph; and in prayerfully examining one in light of the other we may be confident that God will provide us with desperately needed insight into the depths and riches of fatherhood as He Himself lives it and wishes to share it with us. In this way, the allegorical comparison of each patriarch to St. Joseph will be gathered together into one type symbolically directing us toward God's Fatherhood, which alone is capable of showing human fathers how they are to fulfill their vocation to fatherhood.

St. Joseph's fatherhood is the nexus connecting the fathers of old to God's Fatherhood and to our fatherhood. St. Joseph's example will be of great assistance to all fathers who pursue the true and authentic vocation of fatherhood.

---

[6]    Matthew 7:11

# DAY 3

In her litany of praise to St. Joseph, the Church bestows upon the humble carpenter from Nazareth the glorious yet mysterious title, "Light of Patriarchs." The scriptural texts which speak of St. Joseph are indeed few. In the inspired texts of the Old Testament, however, one can indirectly discover the illustrious figure and his significance to modern man. Perhaps so little is written of St. Joseph for the purpose of enticing man to engage in further study of the hidden, humble saint. Perhaps by peering into the patriarchal past one can understand more clearly the present role of Joseph, the father of the patriarchs, and the secrets his example discloses to humanity. If a man dives into the great oceans of meaning within this illustrious title, "Light of Patriarchs," he will gain the ability to discover the great treasures hidden in Joseph, who is himself hidden in the ancient sacred texts. "Therefore every scribe who has been trained for the kingdom of heaven is like a householder who brings out of his treasure what is new and what is old."[7]

Indeed, this virtuous saint illumines the way by which man may peer into the history of the Hebrew generations, revealing, by means of his character, some of the deepest truths contained within the lives of the patriarchs. Planted deep within the example of the patriarchal fathers Abraham, Jacob, Moses, and David, is the hidden seed of Joseph, and in the person of Joseph, the purpose and

---

[7] Matthew 13:52

mission of the patriarchal fathers come to full bloom. The fathers of old foreshadow Joseph, the new father, and in the new fatherhood of Joseph the secrets of old are revealed.

"From the beginning God created man out of his own generosity, He chose the patriarchs to give them salvation. He took his people in hand, teaching them, unteachable as they were, to follow him."[8] Through the patriarchs, those fathers of old, God chose to reveal Himself, His own Fatherhood, and His eternal love for His children. By transmitting the love of God, each in its own way, the lives of the ancient patriarchs foreshadow the exemplar father to come, the one who was chosen to father Christ. In partial and fragmented ways, God chose to speak of his fatherhood through the patriarchs, but in Joseph God revealed His divine Fatherhood in a more evident and excellent way. The humble father of Jesus became an icon of the heavenly Father: a true expression of the Heavenly Father's love for His Son. Indeed, Joseph gathered the lesser lights of the Patriarchs into his own light—an intense light which reveals the Light of lights.

---

[8]    Saint Irenaeus, bishop, *Against Heresies* (125-202)

# DAY 4

---

This Light of Patriarchs streams in three directions. First, Joseph, the Light of Patriarchs, sheds light upon the ancient patriarchs' intense discernments, struggles, and successes, and in particular their vocation of fatherhood. Cast upon the ancient patriarchs of Israel, Joseph's light illuminates the secrets of the vocation of fatherhood and the path to holiness contained therein. By peering into the patriarchal past through the lens of St. Joseph, one can discover that Abraham's Prayer of Faith, Jacob's Prayer of Perseverance, Moses' Prayer of Meditation, and David's Prayer of a King, are all limited types of Joseph's life, which was suffused with prayer, particularly in his discernment of the vocation to marriage and fatherhood. Each of these prayers will furnish the materials for one volume of meditation. Together, these letters will guide us through a progression of steps, drawing us more deeply into a Josephine vision of fatherhood.

Though the patriarchs' example of prayerful discernment was certainly not perfect, each in fragmented ways began to compose a symphony of prayer, comprised of different harmonies which culminated in the score of Joseph's life. Abraham, called by God to leave his fatherland and sacrifice his only son, embraces the virtue of faith; Jacob, threatened by fear and doubt, embraces perseverance, otherwise known as fortitude, animated by the virtue of hope. Adopting the child Israel, Moses renounces his former life in Egypt in exchange for a life of leadership fueled by meditation; and David, who desired to build a house for the

Lord but was denied permission to do so, is called by God, as an expression of love, to provide the materials for this work to his son. Each of these men was called by God to renounce what was useless and embrace that which would aid him in achieving God's will. Joseph harmonized the journeys of his preceding fathers into a journey of his very own. Viewed in this light, the patriarchs reveal the power and glory of Joseph's vocation as father of the Son of God.

Second, this light of wisdom flows from Joseph not only in the direction of the past, but also in the direction of the future. By encountering the just and prayerful man Joseph, you, my brother, will encounter the great patriarchs; and by studying the spiritual journey of these patriarchs, you will not only encounter Joseph, but also come to know yourself, your own fatherhood, and your own sonship. The light of Joseph's discernment reveals the wisdom of the ancient fathers, and the fathers, illuminated by Joseph, cast light upon Joseph himself. All of this reveals Joseph in a clear and instructing light, which ultimately elevates the vocation of fatherhood to its proper status, confirming that this vocation is truly worthy of man and his dignity, and ought to be lauded as such. The illuminated example of fatherhood, exemplified in St. Joseph, is certainly the light of the patriarchs of the past; but it is also the light for future patriarchs living amidst the temptations of the modern world. Finally, this light also streams from Joseph toward heaven, helping the earthly father see the heavenly Father in a clearer light by means of Joseph's fatherhood.

The just, contemplative Joseph is a light for men who are discerning their vital role in God's salvific plan. Marriage and fatherhood are not accidents which simply occur within the history of mankind, but rather realities which God constituted as vocations: paths to holiness, paths to God.

# DAY 5

If the modern Christian man desires to become a scribe who writes the history of his own life, he should be as a wise householder bringing out what is old and new in the art of fatherhood from the treasury of the Light of Patriarchs. Joseph is the householder who, from heaven, desires to bring each of his children great spiritual treasures, both old and new, always pointing men to the eternal Fatherhood of God. In fact, St. Joseph is providentially positioned to help us integrate the wisdom of the Old and New Testaments. Truly, "This just man, who bore within himself the entire heritage of the Old Covenant, was also brought into the 'beginning' of the New and Eternal Covenant in Jesus Christ."[9]

The example of the Light of Patriarchs affords one the ability not only to peer into the past, but, by seeing with the light of Joseph, to see more clearly the Light of Christ. First one peers into the patriarchal past, revealing the prayers of the patriarchs, and also precisely Who they were praying for: namely, Christ. Second, one sees, through the life of Joseph, the Christ child come and submit Himself in obedience to an earthly father, disclosing the eternal value and indescribable importance of fatherhood. When these two visions are combined, we are granted insight into the essential role of fatherhood and its relation to the salvific work of Christ, the eternal Temple: namely, to raise children to become temples of sacrifice. This prayerful vision of the earthly father of Jesus enables fathers

---

[9] Pope John Paul II, *Redemptoris Custos*, 32

to see Christ more clearly as the Son Who directs us to the love of the eternal Father. In our times, God is elevating the father Joseph as the 'Light of Patriarchs' in order to elevate men to their fatherly dignity and ultimately to knowledge of His eternal Fatherhood.

"I am convinced that by reflecting upon the way that Mary's spouse shared the divine mystery, the Church—on the road towards the future with all humanity—will be enabled to discover ever anew her own identity within this redemptive plan, which is founded on the mystery of the Incarnation."[10] Perhaps fathers more than anyone else will discover their essential role in the economy of salvation by reflecting upon the spirituality of fatherhood as seen through this Light of Patriarchs. Perhaps you, my brother, by means of the fatherhood of Joseph, will discover the secret to masculinity, fatherhood, prayer, and self-sacrificial love; perhaps in discovering these secrets you will discover the God Who loves you from all of eternity; and perhaps in finding this love you will discover your own purpose within the cosmos.

---

[10]    Pope John Paul II, *Redemptoris Custos*, 1

# DAY 6

## THE GLORIOUS DEFICIENCY OF FATHERHOOD

Often, when we ponder the lives of the saints, those heroes and heroines who defended and proclaimed the faith of Christ and His Church with self-sacrifice and ardor, we envision a virgin martyr, a priest, a sister, perhaps a hermit, a brother, an apostle, or one of the apostles' successors. With the exception of the Blessed Mother and St. Joseph, infrequently does a saint who was betrothed in marriage come to mind. Although many married saints have been canonized, whose example the Church lauds and extols, and though there have existed saints who were also fathers, there are few in comparison to those who lived a celibate life; and of these fatherly saints, even fewer are lauded precisely for their fatherhood.

This lack of recognition of the human father initially appears to indicate a great deficiency in fatherhood as a means of pursuing holiness. Often a father believes that being married and having children hinders him, if it does not altogether disqualify him, from achieving great sanctity. He may even conclude that sainthood is impossible for him, and rather than pursuing radical holiness, he compromises with worldly whims and diversions, expecting little from himself or from God. This, my brother, is a scandal to the vocation of fatherhood.

While it is true that "He who is married is concerned about the things of the world, how he may please his wife; and he is divided,"[11]

---

[11]   See 1 Corinthians 7:10

the same apostle also said, "Let every man remain in the calling in which he was called. If thou cannot be free"—that is, not married—"make use of it [marriage] rather."[12]

The married man and the father is beset by many challenges, for he is one who must "live in the world and not [be] of the world,"[13] and is therefore tempted gravely in varying ways. Yet if a father is wise, he can make use of his vocational call, which is good, sacred, and issues from God, and thereby journey on the path of becoming an icon of the heavenly Father. In doing so he even has the great potential of directing humanity to the Father. My fellow father, though being a father may appear to be a great impediment in your pursuit of sainthood, in your endeavor to achieve great holiness, you are nevertheless called to use this weakness to achieve this worthy and attainable goal.

How can a deficiency be used in attaining a goal? How can an apparently weak vocation enable one to embrace sainthood?

Let us reflect upon the words of St. Paul:

> And lest the greatness of the revelations should puff me up, there was given me a thorn in the flesh, a messenger of Satan, to buffet me. Concerning this I thrice besought the Lord that it might leave me. And He said to me, 'My grace is sufficient for thee, for strength is made perfect in weakness.' Gladly therefore I will glory in my infirmities that the strength of God dwell in me....For when I am weak, then I am strong.[14]

My brother, human fatherhood is indeed a great gift. In fact, in its essence it constitutes a type of revelation of God's Fatherhood given to the world, but more particularly to fathers. The greatness of fatherhood was exercised in a limited yet powerful way in the

---

[12]   1 Corinthians 7:20

[13]   See Romans 12:2

[14]   2 Corinthians 12:9

lives of the patriarchs. Throughout the ages, however, men have often reduced human fatherhood, which ought to be an image of God's Fatherhood, to male tyranny. Today, many have discarded the good of fatherhood because of those fathers who abused their fatherhood, and, thinking they are righteous in discarding father-hood, they unwittingly deny the Father Who created fatherhood. This rejection of fatherhood constitutes a thorn in the flesh of fatherhood, a message from Satan, which buffets the good of father-hood, contributing to the impression that the vocation is inferior and even a hindrance to sanctity.

The Lord, however, does not reject fatherhood, though He does reject the abuse of fatherly authority. Therefore, like St. Paul, we fathers must admit our weakness, confess that we are divided in many ways, that we are tempted by the world to misuse or neglect our gift of fatherhood, and by this confession allow God to apply the grace necessary to restore fatherhood to its true, good, and noble condition. By accepting the deficiency or weakness of the vocation of fatherhood, we allow God to demonstrate His strength, using fatherhood as means to redeem and sanctify, to transform sinful men into saintly fathers.

Let us also recall St. Thérèse, who longed to become a mis-sionary, a doctor of the Church, a teacher and Apostle, and yet, by means of her consecrated vocation, was seemingly constrained by the walls of her cell from achieving her heart's desire. Thérèse expressed the inner pain she endured from this "thorn" of defi-ciency, this apparent limitedness of her vocation. In embracing this pain, while remaining confident that her desires were divinely inspired, she received the Sacred Revelation: "And I point out to you a more excellent way...The greatest of these [ways] is love."[15]

The young saint discovered that her vocation was love, that in love she should be the very heart of the Church. By following this

---

[15]    1 Corinthians 13:1; 1 Corinthians 13:13

greatest, most excellent way she became teacher, apostle, missionary, and doctor of the Church, honors bestowed upon her to this day.

My brother, the apparent deficiencies of fatherhood, its apparent inability to "sell all," "give all," and "be all" for the Lord, can indeed appear to be an insurmountable weakness. Yet if we truly become fathers, we do indeed sell all: that is, we cast out worldly temptations in exchange for a life of familial communion, which is an iconic reminder and even a participation in the eternal exchange of love of the Triune God. We do indeed give all: that is, we pass on all the resources we receive from God to our wife and children. We do indeed become all, by being a father who is an icon of the Heavenly Father of all, while also being a son who is dependent upon the Father and His begotten Son, Who is Savior of all; and by being teachers inspired with the charity and wisdom of the Advocate, the Holy Spirit, the Teacher of all.

Our Lord confirms the vitality of fatherhood with these words:

> Amen I say to you, unless you turn and become like little children you will not enter the kingdom of heaven. Whoever, therefore, humbles himself as this little child, he is greatest in the kingdom of heaven. And whoever receives one such little child for My sake, receives Me.[16]

My fellow father, understand how your vocation of fatherhood is properly disposed to the call to greatness. A father becomes like a little child by recognizing his own dependence upon the Father, precisely in his desire to provide for the child he has received. A father who humbles himself can, through Christ the Son, become a son of God, by means of receiving a little child and becoming a father for the sake of Christ. Indeed, the rewards of the vocation of fatherhood which Christ promises are among the greatest: "Whoever therefore humbles himself like a little child, he is greatest

---

[16]    Matthew 18:3-5

in the kingdom of heaven." And again, "whoever receives one such little child for my sake, receives Me." A father who humbles himself in this way will be able to say, with St. Paul, "In my infirmities the strength of God dwells in me."

The weakness and deficiency of fatherhood demand that you, my fellow father, become humble, little, lowly, and dependent upon God the Father, while also demanding that you become a great father of your domestic church. By receiving a child, you, my brother, will become a father, while also becoming a child by becoming dependent upon the Father. By becoming a father, small and humble, you will be among the greatest in the kingdom, inheriting Christ Himself!

My brother, let us study the life of St. Joseph, who was both son of the Father and father of the Son, and become as he became.

.

PRAYER OF FAITH

# DAY 7

Every man hopes. Often man has hopes which appear worldly, such as aspirations for a beautiful home, a successful career, or to remain young, active and alive. At the center of these temporal hopes, however, there lies a deeper and purer hope, which perhaps has become misguided or disordered. For example, the hope for a beautiful home indicates a deeper desire for the perfect home of heaven. The hope for a successful career indicates that within a man there exists the altruistic hope of being glorified by glorifying God. The desire to remain young, active and alive is an indication of the noble longing for eternal life.

In the depth of his being, man consciously or unconsciously hopes for eternal life, eternal Love—a life lived in eternal union with God, the only Being Who can completely fulfill him. The fact that, in the face of all his accomplishments, man longs for more, proves that there is a More to be longed for, and this More is God.

A man may desire power or to be powerful, which indicates a deeper hope for the supernatural power of God to reign within him, to inspire him, and give him the strength to move beyond himself and become the man, the father, he hopes to be; and more importantly, the man and the father whom God calls him to be.

The reason we have disordered desires is because we cannot see the true good, except with the eyes of faith. Faith gives us the eyes to see what we cannot see and obtain what cannot be obtained in this world.

Faith believes that the aforementioned hopes are substantial, real, and can, by the power of God, be fully realized within the human person. Such faith justifies a man in the sight of the perfect God,[17] enabling him to perform, as a child of the Father, the works of the Father in his own fatherhood. Our Lord revealed this truth to his disciples: "In this is my Father glorified, that you may bear very much fruit, and become my disciples."[18] The faith of an imperfect man in the Perfect God justifies that man, granting his faith real power to accomplish the works of God, for "faith without works is dead."[19] By believing in God and the Son He sent, the man of faith "can do all things in Christ Who strengthens him."[20]

To become a faithful father, a man must possess the gift of faith, the gift of believing and trusting in God as his loving Father. But how can the human father obtain faith and trust in God's love? God the Father did what no earthly father is capable of doing: He expressed His undying, relentless love for hardened sinners, by means of the complete self-donation and sacrifice of His Son. Because of this sacrifice we can have faith in His love for us. By believing and trusting that God the Father gave His own Son over to man, fathers will be given the faith necessary to give their own children to God freely, which is the ultimate goal of fatherhood. This giving of one's own child to the Father is the work, the fruit, which faith produces in a father.

Faith, "the substance of things hoped for, the evidence of things unseen,"[21] is the key which unlocks the treasures of God's benevolence. In fact, God is complete Gift and completely spends Himself, pouring Himself out on behalf of man, giving to man His greatest gift, namely Himself. The unlimited generosity of the unseen God

---

[17]   See Romans 4:5
[18]   John 15:8
[19]   James 2:24
[20]   See Philippians 4:13
[21]   Hebrews 11:1

is fully expressed, given to us, and seen in His Son Jesus Christ, and it is faith which grants us access to receive this already given Gift.

My brother, your vocation as a father is dependent upon and must be founded upon faith, which is a "personal adherence to God."[22] This adherence consists of submitting your fatherhood to, and trusting in, the true Father, the God of Heaven, for without this trustful, filial submission, "it is impossible to please God."[23]

The man who lives and fathers from the foundation of faith moves from the sphere of pride, which is expressed in radical individualism, selfishness, and mistrust of and doubt in God's generosity, to a disposition of dependence upon God, believing and trusting that God is the generous Father Who provides for His children. This act of belief is more than an intellectual act, but rather a complete abandonment of the entire will and person to God, believing that His ways are better than our ways.

The Prayer of Faith is the first of the four foundational pillars that support the structure of the temple, the house, that is, the very being of the human father. A father's life is a life of prayer given, offered, and sacrificed to the Heavenly Father, and the first pillar of this life of prayer is the Prayer of Faith.

The Prayer of Faith is comprised of three components: silence, obedience and sacrifice. The first component, silence before God, affords man the opportunity to listen and hear God's call in his life, to receive divine guidance and direction as to how he should properly respond to the call to fatherly greatness.

Silence is itself comprised of three parts. First is the habit of active listening, that is, the act of embracing silence before God, in order to hear God. Second is the decision to be known rather than noticed, that is, to overcome the grave temptation of vainglory, of longing to be accepted by men, of desiring self-exaltation or the

---

[22]   CCC 150

[23]   CCC 161

praise of others, instead of choosing to know God and be known by God. The authentic man, rather than being noticed by man, becomes known by God. Third is the characteristic of secrecy, an imitation of the hiddenness of the Heavenly Father, Who accomplishes all things in secret.

The second component of the Prayer of Faith is Obedience, itself also comprised of three parts. The first aspect of Obedience is a proof of faith which is the direct result of listening. For if a man has faith, he listens to God, and such listening presupposes that he is ready and willing to act upon what he hears, to respond to the direction received, to obey.

The second component of obedience flows from this proof of faith, and is demonstrated in the father's deliberate decision to reconcile with and dedicate himself to his vocation. This decision is a deliberate act of continually and wholeheartedly receiving his wife, along with the offspring she bears, as his own God-given responsibility, a responsibility which should never be cast aside.

The third mark of obedience is enduring a test of faith, which always entails some type of sacrifice and marks a turning point in a man's life.

The third component of the Prayer of Faith includes a particular type of sacrifice on the part of the father in fidelity to God. This is comprised of three stages: the initiating stage, when the father initiates his child in the way of sacrifice by means of laying upon the child's back the wood of the cross, that is, the wood of discipline. The second stage of sacrifice is the unitive stage, when, rather than abandoning his child to learn the art of sacrifice alone, the father unites himself to his child, dedicating himself to assisting the child in bearing the cross of self-sacrifice. The third stage of sacrifice is the vicarious stage, which means that the father cannot complete his child's personal sacrifice, nor does he have the right to do so. Rather, by offering himself for his child, the father inspires his child and so lives on vicariously in the child's own self-offering.

Silence, marked by obedience, expressed in sacrificial love for one's own child, comprises the Prayer of Faith, the essential, fundamental and initial pillar of a father's life of prayer.

To more effectively and vividly describe the Prayer of Faith, and in order to penetrate its essential value in the endeavor of becoming a truly faith-filled father, we will briefly examine the faithful example of Abraham and typologically compare his faith to that of Joseph, the father of Jesus.[24] We will particularly examine, first, how God called each of them within his own personal, silent, solitude, encouraging each of them to abandon fear and trust wholeheartedly in the Lord; second, how God encouraged them to demonstrate belief in His promises by obediently embracing the responsibility of his vocation; and third, how He called them to sacrifice obediently the fruits of the promise received by returning those fruits to God.

By means of these two patriarchs, Abraham and Joseph, we will discover our own need for faith, recover our fatherly responsibility for our vocation, and ultimately achieve an understanding of our role, as fathers, to surrender our children, in sacrifice, to the Lord. Indeed, "the just man lives by faith,"[25] and Abraham, as our "father in faith,"[26] and "Joseph as a just man,"[27] together provide guidance for fathers seeking to live by the theological virtue of faith.

---

[24]   See Matthew 13:55

[25]   See Romans

[26]   See Hebrews

[27]   See Matthew 1:19

*Silence*

# DAY 8

Silence is among the greatest treasures and most necessary commodities. So precious is silence that one must actively pursue it, strategizing to determine ways to abide in the peace and stillness silence has to offer. Bombarded by the ever multiplying voices of our age, the ears of today's father more readily hear the gospel of the world and follow such worldly advice, rarely possessing the space and time to hear the God of the true Gospel, a Gospel of radical liberation and profound interior healing.

Silence opens a man's heart and mind to hearing the silent voice of God, Whose "first language is silence."[28] To become like God we must know God, to know God we must be able to communicate with Him, and to communicate with Him we must speak His language, the language of silence.

To speak with God demands that we humble ourselves before God. As the psalmist, speaking of God, states, "Sacrifice and holocausts You do not desire, but an open ear."[29] Silently listening to God is the sacrifice of the heart, a sacrifice which is acceptable to God. The sacrifice of an open ear silences pride, rendering the person capable of hearing the voice of God. By hearing the voice of God, a man will learn God's holy will, and will be more capable of obeying it.

---

[28]    St. John of the Cross

[29]    Psalm 39:6

The words of the psalmist, "I delight to do Thy will, O my God; Thy law is written upon my heart,"[30] remind us that by opening our ear to God we allow God to write His law, His love, His ways upon our hearts, making us capable of pleasing Him.

The law cannot be reduced to the commandments given to Moses on Sinai, but rather should be understood in light of these words of Christ: "Truly I say to you, he who hears My Word and believes the Father Who sent me has eternal life."[31] And again our Lord said, "Every one who hears these words of Mine and does them will be like a wise man who built his house upon rock....it did not fall because it had been founded upon the rock."[32]

The wise man, the wise father, opens his ear to the Words of Christ with the intention of obeying them, and such obedience will grant success to his vocation. However, to hear the Word demands silence, and the language of silence poses a great challenge for the human father. And yet, if a father desires this treasure, he will sacrifice the voices of the world, more and more, to attain it.

Indeed, to enter into silence with God presupposes the gift of faith. A man who is decidedly silent before God is a man who waits upon his Father, trusting with faith that God will direct his life's course. In fact, silence is a key characteristic of a man who fears neither the rejection of men, nor the absence of man's worldly messages, but rather fears the Lord. Such a man humbles himself before God, acknowledging and believing that the words of God are more precious than the words of men. Such a man does not rely upon worldly remedies or worldly advice to his difficult situations, but rather submits himself to God, presenting his dilemma to the Father, and with faith patiently waits for divine direction.

---

[30]   Psalm 39:8

[31]   See John 5:24

[32]   Matthew 7:24-25

My brother, to obtain the wisdom of God, His voice must be heard, and to hear His voice speaking within your heart, you must embrace silence. It is in silence that God speaks, and without sound His voice is heard. As previously stated, sacrifice is demanded of the one who desires to hear the voice of God; indeed, silence is one of the many deaths to self that eventually gives birth to a vibrant life of faith.

The heavenly Father invites all fathers to enter into His silence, that they may become like Him and image His Fatherhood to the fallen world. If a man declines this invitation to silence, he rejects the possibility of obtaining a deep and abiding faith, a faith which unlocks the treasures of God's generosity.

One reason men so often decline God's invitation to silence is to the lack of a deep, interior trust in God. This distrust creates a fundamental disquiet in the soul, convincing many men that God will not speak in the silence. Man therefore turns to other, more stimulating ways to access what he believes is God's message.

Though these other means may indeed transmit the message of God, silence is the foundation of any genuine appropriation of this message, and without silence a man has great difficulty determining whether or not these stimulating transmissions are of God or not; or, more importantly, whether a given message is given by God to him in particular.

# DAY 9

The first component of Silence is listening, being ready, actively waiting for direction in one's vocation. Listening is so essential to the formation of the soul that our Lord's ministry began and ended with miraculous signs related to man's need to listen.

Christ's public ministry opened at the wedding of Cana in Galilee, when the servants whom He commanded to obtain the water to become wine were first commanded by His Mother to "do whatever he tells you."[33] In other words, Our Lady commanded the servants to listen to and obey Jesus' command. This miracle occurred not only because of Mary's concern for the couple, but also because of the servants' ability to listen to what Christ commanded them to do. Because the servants listened and obeyed, our Lord transformed their work into wine.

At the close of Christ's public ministry, in the Garden of Gethsemane, when Judas and the cohort came in the darkness of night to arrest Jesus, "Simon Peter, . . . having a sword, drew it and struck the servant of the high priest and cut off his right ear."[34] But Jesus "touched his ear and healed him."[35] This healing of Malchus' ear was the last of Christ's public miracles, indicating the significance of Christ's desire to restore our ability to "listen to Him."

---

[33]   John 2:5
[34]   John 18:10
[35]   Luke 22:51

Listening to God is so essential to our spiritual well being that our Lord bookended his public ministry with these two miracles, indicating that God desires our hearing to be healed that we may "listen to Him."[36]

Listening does not necessarily indicate an absence of thoughts or words. Traditional prayers, meditation upon the Sacred Scriptures, praying the Liturgy, and praising God spontaneously are essential for a fruitful prayer life. Indeed, we ought to listen to these words expressed by mouth or mind and meditate upon them deeply, waiting upon God to direct our hearts.

Yet the movement from exterior modes of prayer to an interior silence before God is essential for our prayer life, and it is because of our need to listen that the evil one tempts us to remain upon the surface of prayer without diving beneath its surface and penetrating the ocean of God and His mystery.

The man who has faith will consistently strive to overcome such temptations, understanding that the One Whose Presence he is in is the God of wisdom, and it is this Word Who fills the minds of men who are willing to overcome the temptation to fill prayer with idle words.

God the Father initiates dialogue with you, my brother, prompting you to respond to his invitation to intimacy, to silence, to listening. After we have addressed God, we ought to enter into silent receptivity, actively listening, waiting for the voice of God spoken within us. During this period of prayer we may be tempted to flee from the silence and the posture of listening, and instead default to using external forms of prayer, which often are filled with words, hoping that these words will grant us some form of consolation. However, if God is calling us to silent receptivity and active listening, such a response will deflect the generosity of God, and

---

[36]   Mark 9:6

rather than progressing spiritually, we will weaken in our ability to listen to God, and thus lose our peace.

God is often ready to give us wisdom and peace if we remain receptive and reflective, awaiting Him, even  and especially when we do not perceive His voice.

As the Lord said to the people of Israel, "Listen to my voice, and do all that I command you. So shall you be my people, and I will be your God."[37] Notice, my brother, that in order to become God's own child, to have the Spirit of God's Fatherhood animating our fatherhood, we must first listen to His voice. Such listening enables the human father to hear the voice of the Father in heaven, prompting him to obey God's commands.

Listening and obedience are two sides of the same coin; they can scarcely be separated; for obedience is the first fruit of listening and obedience presupposes that one is listening.

Silence may initially appear to have a passive character, but if we understand silence as listening, we discover that listening is active silence, a purposeful disposition of readiness before God. My brother, let us now examine the model presented by Abraham and Joseph as they waited silently upon God.

---

[37]    Jeremiah 11:4

# DAY 10

## The Listening Heart of Abraham

We first encounter the man Abram in the twelfth chapter of Genesis, where he is called by God to leave the land of his kindred and move to a land that God would eventually show him.

> When God calls him, Abraham goes forth as the Lord has told him (Gen 12:4). Abraham's heart was entirely submissive to the Word and so he obeys. Such attentiveness of the heart, whose decisions are made according to God's will, is essential to prayer, while words used count only in relation to it.[38]

In fact, the first three chapters describing Abram's life contain only the words of God and the silent obedience of Abram. This silence on Abram's part speaks in a powerful manner of the attentiveness of Abram's heart, which waited upon the Lord's direction, and after receiving this direction from the Lord, obediently complied. Indeed, "Abraham's prayer is expressed first by deeds; a man of silence, he constructs an altar to the Lord at each stage of his journey."[39]

> Only later (in the fifteenth chapter of Genesis) does Abraham's first prayer comprised of words appear: a veiled complaint reminding God of his promises which seem unfulfilled. Thus one aspect of the drama

---

[38]  CCC 2570

[39]  ibid

of prayer appears from the beginning: the test of faith in the fidelity of God.[40]

Abram's faith indeed was challenged. The meaning of the name Abram was "high father," and yet Abram did not have any offspring to demonstrate his worthiness of the vocational title of father, let alone high father. This appears to be something that Abram, within the silence of his personal solitude, meditated upon at length; for the fifteenth chapter opens by telling us that "the Word of the Lord came to Abram by a vision saying 'Fear not Abram, I am your shield, and thy reward shall be very great.'"[41]

God's words to Abram indicate that Abram in his mediations has become fearful; but what did Abram fear? In the preceding chapter, Abram rescued his nephew Lot after he had been captured during the invasion of his land by the four kings; by "dividing his company, he rushed upon them in the night and defeated them."[42] Abram was obviously no longer afraid of his enemies, for he was a man of great courage, which was proved in the pursuing and slaughtering of those enemies who had captured Lot. What then did Abram fear?

Within the heart of the aging Abram was the overwhelming fear that he would not have a son of his own. Even more perplexing was that God had promised Abram, "I will make of thee a great nation, and I will bless thee, and magnify thy name, and thou shalt be blessed."[43]

Indeed, God promised to make of Abram a great nation and to magnify his name, "high father," meaning that Abraham would beget a nation by means of becoming a father and having offspring of his own. This fear of God not fulfilling His promises is reflected

---

[40]   ibid

[41]   Genesis 15:1

[42]   Genesis 14:15

[43]   Genesis 15:2-3

in Abram's response to God: "Lord God, what will Thou give me? I shall go without children, and the son of the steward of my house is this Damascus Eliezar. And Abram added: But to me Thou has not given seed; and lo, my servant, born in my house, shall be my heir."[44]

This prayerful dialogue between God and Abram began within the context of Abram's silent meditation upon his fearful and apparently hopeless situation. Abram, in his vocational crisis, appeared passive, and yet he was not without action, but rather actively waited upon God, silently presenting his fears to the Lord.

In his ready and watchful silence, God approached Abram, initiating His plan, granting Abram vocational direction. God spoke to Abram His word because Abram listened: "And immediately the Word of the Lord came to him saying, 'He shall not be thy heir; but he that shall come out of thy bowels, him thou shall have for thy heir.'"[45]

My brother, learn from Abram that God grants guidance and direction to the man of silence, who actively listens, who waits and is ready to obey the Lord.

After the Lord made the promise to Abram that a child from his own seed should be his heir, God opened Abram's heart to the mystery of faith, bringing him outside and saying,

> "Look toward heaven and number the stars if you are able to number them." Then He said to him, "So shall your descendants be." And he believed the Lord; and he reckoned it to him as righteousness.[46]

Later, within the same account, the Scripture discloses that the Lord had actually commanded Abram to count the stars while it was daylight, which rendered the stars imperceptible. Though Abram could see, he was blind to what existed in the heavens, and

---

[44]   ibid

[45]   Genesis 15:4

[46]   Genesis 15:6

yet he gave his assent of faith, believing not in what was seen but what was unseen.

Seeing with his own eyes that he had no offspring, Abram relied upon his eyes of faith, believing in the promise of what was unseen instead of what was seen, and because of this God reckoned it to him as righteousness, for "what is seen is temporary, but what is unseen is eternal."[47] Because of his faith, Abram became the "father of many nations,"[48] for "in view of the promise of God, he did not waver through unbelief, but was strengthened in faith, giving glory to God, being fully aware that whatever God has promised He is able to perform."[49]

My brother, faith is needed to grow in silence before God, and silence before God enables one to grow in faith. God initially tests a man by calling him to exercise faith and enter into receptive silence, asking him to listen to His interior voice. After a man has demonstrated his faithfulness to such silence, God further tests the man's faith in His invitation, which usually involves some type of promise. God has many promises, many gifts, which he desires to bestow upon your fatherhood, and yet He is calling you to enter into faithful silence, listening and waiting. This, my brother, is the initial step of faith which sets the trajectory of your vocation toward holy success and glorification of God the Father.

---

[47]    2 Corinthians 4:18

[48]    Genesis 17:5

[49]    Romans 4:20

# DAY 11

The Church in her litany of praise and honor of St. Joseph lauds the humble carpenter of Nazareth as "Joseph most faithful." This hidden, humble, silent carpenter is understood and extolled by the Church as not only a faithful man, but also a man preeminently faithful. For this reason Joseph is a profound typological fulfillment of Abraham, our "father in faith."[50]

If Abraham is our father in faith, Joseph is our father most faithful. Joseph is a father among fathers, an example of faith among the faithful, and therefore is a resplendent example of faith for each and every father who desires to become a faithful father.

As we will see, my brother, Joseph's fatherhood is a fitting example of faith and the fulfillment of Abraham's faith because of his silence, obedience, and sacrificial love. The first of these admirable characteristics of faith, silence, is expressed profoundly in the life of Joseph, a man who waited upon the Word of God to direct his actions.

The Sacred Scriptures contain very few passages that directly speak of St. Joseph, yet although the sacred texts speak so infrequently of Joseph, we may discover the secrets of living a "life of greatness"[51] by listening to what the Scriptures do not directly declare and thus understanding more clearly what the Word is declaring. The very silence in Sacred Scripture with regards to

---

[50] See Romans 3:27
[51] Pope Paul VI

Joseph declares to us that the hidden, silent, humble example of Joseph is an essential characteristic of fatherhood.

We first encounter the silent Joseph in St. Matthew's genealogy of Jesus. This genealogy begins with Abraham, the father of our faith, and ends with the faithful Joseph, the legal father of Jesus.[52] This genealogy is a genealogy of fatherhood beginning with Abraham who was "justified by faith"[53] and completed by Joseph, "the just man"[54] who "lived by faith."[55] In a profound way, this genealogy calls upon all fathers to imitate the examples of these two faith-filled men whose silence is worthy of imitation.

As with his typological predecessor Abram, we encounter Joseph during the storm of a vocational crisis. Recall, my brother, that Abram's name, "high father," indicated the identity of his vocation. Likewise, Joseph's name "comes from the verb 'yasab' meaning to add, increase, do again... The name Joseph means Increaser, Repeater, and Doubler. He shall add."[56]

Joseph's name also provides a clue to his life's vocation and saintly identity. Joseph, Son of David, was a direct descendent of the Davidic line, and therefore had received a royal heritage and ancestry that gave him the potential to be a king, though he remained hidden and unnoticed. Joseph silently carried this secret of his royal inheritance; yet being a direct descendant of David, a just man, and a faithful Jew, he surely longed, with all of Israel, for the advent of the long expected Messiah, from Whom would come descendants more numerous than the stars.

Indeed, part of this consideration must have been the possibility that Joseph himself could marry and have offspring, and that one of

---

[52]   See Matthew 1:1-16

[53]   See Romans 5:1

[54]   See Matthew 1:19

[55]   See Romans 1:17

[56]   Abarim Publications, http://www.abarim-publications.com/Meaning/Joseph.html#.UotzvsSko3l

those male children could become the long awaited Messiah. This ability to transfer the kingship of David was a gift given by God to Joseph, and the potential of this gift was a reality that Joseph, at some level, must have considered.

Considering this potential, Joseph's name has tremendous significance. The potential of providing an heir to the Davidic Throne would indeed fulfill the meaning of "he shall add"; for Joseph would be adding to the line of Davidic Kings. This potential increased when Joseph betrothed Mary, the humble young virgin of Nazareth.

As with Abram, however, we encounter Joseph in a seemingly impossible situation. Mary, the soon to be Mother of the Messiah, "had been betrothed to Joseph, before they came together, (and) she was found to be with child by the Holy Spirit. But Joseph being a just man and not wishing to expose her to shame, was minded to put her away privately. But while he considered this, behold an angel of the Lord appeared to him in a dream, saying, "Do not be afraid Joseph, son of David."[57]

Notice, my brother, Joseph's profound silence before the Lord. Joseph offered no verbal prayer, made no outcry, and he voiced no plea; amidst the intensity and tension of the tumultuous situation, he simply presented his dilemma before the Lord. Joseph's silence before God presupposes that he had a holy fear of, and great faith in, God, believing that God would supply a resolution to his dilemma.

Indeed, Joseph did not seek man's counsel to remedy the situation, but rather abided in faith, in a holy fear of God, and actively waited upon the Lord, trusting that his God would direct him.

Joseph's silence indicates his listening disposition, a spirit of readiness, of waiting to be directed and guided in his vocation. As with Abraham, in the midst of faith-filled silence, the Word of the

---

[57] Matthew 1:18-20

Lord came to Joseph: "Joseph, Son of David, do not fear."[58] Just as the Lord encouraged Abram, "fear not Abram, I am your shield,"[59] so the Lord also encouraged the "just man," Joseph, for whom He fulfilled the promise given to the psalmist, to "bless him who is just: with [His] goodwill, as with a shield, [to] surround him."[60]

Abram and Joseph, both being just, and both being men of faith, are protected by God as with a shield, and therefore are encouraged by God to "be not afraid." Indeed, like Abraham, God came to Joseph in silence because Joseph listened, and made a promise to Joseph much like the promise He made to Abram:

"Sarah, your wife, shall bear you a son and you shall call him Isaac. I will establish my covenant with him as an everlasting covenant."[61]

"Take to thee Mary thy wife, for that which is begotten of her is of the Holy Spirit. And she shall bring forth a Son, and thou shall call His name Jesus; for He shall save His people from their sins."[62]

Each man is promised that his wife will bring forth a son, each is told to name the son, and each is told the role he will play in salvation history: namely, that in him an everlasting covenant will be established. Through Joseph's faithful fatherhood, even more than through Abraham's fatherhood in faith, Jesus comes to establish the new and everlasting covenant in His own blood, a covenant for all. [63]

Like Abram, Joseph was asked by God to look into the heavens, beyond an apparently hopeless situation, and count the stars in the sky, that is, to believe in the promise that the "child conceived in

[58]   Matthew 1:20

[59]   Genesis 15:1

[60]   Psalm 5

[61]   Genesis 17:19

[62]   Matthew 1: 20-21

[63]   See Luke 22:20 and Mark 14:24

her is of the Holy Spirit,"[64] and that this child would be "the savior of His people"[65]

My friend, let us learn from Joseph, who, like Abram, exercised tremendous faith, trusting that the Lord would fulfill His promises. As the meaning of Joseph's name suggests, Joseph "repeated" Abraham's faith journey while also "doing this on top of Abraham," that is , he "doubled" the faith of Abraham by receiving God's plan with patient, silent faith.

By believing, Joseph became like Abraham, the "father of many nations,"[66] through Christ, his legal Son, Who made Joseph's descendants "more numerous than the stars."[67]

"In view of the promise of God, he did not waver through unbelief but was strengthened in faith, giving glory to God, being fully aware that whatever God has promised He is able to perform."[68]

My brother, Joseph is our fatherly example, a man who believed in the invisible promise of God, regardless of the visible obstacles that surrounded him. Joseph, by demonstrating great faith, responded to the nagging temptations of doubt by clinging to the Lord in silence, listening, waiting for God's answer; and because of this it was credited to him as righteousness, in his amply deserved titles of "just man" and "most faithful."

You, my brother, in pursuit of fulfilling your vocation of fatherhood, will encounter various trials, obstacles, and nearly impossible situations, and it is amongst all of these that you must exercise the gift of faith, which will shield you from the darts of doubt and lead you to become an expression of the glory of God the Father.

---

[64] Matthew 1: 21

[65] ibid

[66] See Genesis 17:5

[67] Genesis 22

[68] Romans 4:20

# DAY 12

### Being Known rather than Being Noticed

"The deepest desire of the human heart is to know another and be known by another." (St. Augustine) Being known and being noticed by another are very different in meaning. To be known by another demands that we actually give ourselves in service to others for the sake of their unrepeatable person; by giving ourselves to another, we become known (in all sincerity) for who we really are. To know another is to discover the other by loving the person for his or her own sake, and to be known by another is to be loved for the sake of our own person; a person that can only be discovered by means of sincere self-donation.[69]

Often, however, in desiring to be known by another, we may inadvertently fall prey to the temptation to use ourselves, neglecting our own personal dignity by placing ourselves on stage in order to be noticed, using and manipulating the gifts of our bodies, our talents, our person so that others may notice us; being noticed in this way, we are affirmed in a false sense of self-knowledge.

When we act in this manner others do not truly know us, but rather, they know of us, and our true self remains hidden beneath the pseudo-person we desire to make noticed.

My brother, the vocation of fatherhood has been created by God in such a way that it acts as a fire, which burns away the desire to be noticed, while purifying the sincere underlying

---

[69]   See *Gaudium et Spes*, 24

desire to be authentically known. Indeed, the man who endeavors diligently to fulfill the vocation of fatherhood will, at some point in his life, encounter periods of spiritual desolation. Lacking recognition from others, he will be tempted to believe that his life is almost entirely meaningless, and to doubt that he has provided, by means of his hidden, silent, unknown, sacrificial service to his family, anything of true value for God and God's Kingdom.

This grave temptation, if surrendered to at any level, will eventually lead to thoughts or plans to become noticed by others, to become a success by worldly standards; and if these plans are accomplished they will give the man a false sense of fulfillment, recognition, and honor.

My brother, if you judge success and achievement by the world's standard, it is only a matter of time before you will fall prey to this temptation, which will also lead to the eventual neglect of your vocation of fatherhood for the sake of self-exaltation. A father who desires godly success within his vocational mission must instead remember that he cannot accurately measure the success of his own vocation, for it is a continual work of sacrificial love, ending only in death.

Another temptation, perhaps even more harmful due to its alluring and apparently godly character, is the temptation to invest oneself primarily in a ministry beyond that of fatherhood. Such a proposal is a most cunning snare of the enemy, for it has the power to seduce a father into believing that he will be accomplishing a greater good, for example by rebuilding the Church or serving God's people, and that these noble objectives should have pride of place in his heart – even before his service to his family.

The evil one works tirelessly to persuade those who are called to the unnoticed mission of raising a holy family to abandon this mission in order to become noticed by means of public service. Indeed, a father who feels called to public ministry must discern clearly whether or not this calling is from God, or whether it is an evil distraction, luring him away from the God-given task to which he should give his full attention. Many families and marriages have been destroyed because of a father's decision to act upon such temptations.

My brother, be careful to discern clearly such apparent vocations, and be not convinced by mere temptations. The evil one will attempt to convince you to be exteriorly active, seen by others, performing deeds to be seen by men, tempting you to measure your own value based upon what others think of you rather than upon what God knows of you.

A confessor once said, "Do not become a street lamp only to have your house go dark," and another said, "You will become a saint by means of your vocation, not outside of it." Often a father, believing his actions to be Christ-like, performs duties outside of the family for the larger family of God, only to neglect the family entrusted to him. Yet if a father neglects his immediate family, he is ultimately neglecting the larger family of God and doing the Church a great disservice.

My brother, this truth is foundational in restoring the world from its brokenness: The macro-family of the world will begin to be created anew, healed from her brokenness, reconciled in communion, when the Church is renewed; the Church will be renewed when the family becomes healed of division by Christ's redeeming grace; and the micro-church of the family will experience healing and reconciliation when marriages become icons of Christ's marriage to His Church.

The family, the micro-church, by means of its communal harmony, transmits to the world, with a certain iconic eloquence, the message of the inner mystery of the Triune Godhead: the eternal exchange of Persons of the Trinity. Therefore, we fathers ought to work first with God the Father in the project of redeeming our families, and then, once a strong familial communion has been established, we may branch out further by assisting in the projects of the macro-Church.

My brother, if you discover that you are truly called by God to carry out works that place you in the public sphere, strive always to keep in mind that these ministries are secondary to your primary vocation of fatherhood.

Undoubtedly, as you see others performing works of greatness, you will question yourself, wondering if your life has any value in the economy of salvation.

Those called by God to speak to crowds, serve in the mission field, or fulfill apostolates within the context of the local parish, can and often do receive instant gratification.

In comparison, a father intent on his vocation of serving his family may receive very little instantaneous gratification, and seemingly little recognition. This lack of appreciation affords the father the opportunity to please God by exercising great faith, trusting that God will raise holy ones from his very own family, which will help comprise the promised descendants, more numerous than the stars, to fill the ranks of the Church.

My brother, discern your vocation well, and hold fast to the priorities demanded of a father; for the closer someone is to us, the greater the obligation we have to serve them. Serve your family, the micro-church, and by serving your micro-church, you will be participating in the service and mission of the transformation of the macro-family, the universal Church.

My brother, if God has chosen you to become a saint by means of the vocation of fatherhood, believe that "he who began a good work in you will bring it to completion,"[70] regardless of whether or not you are noticed. "God will never inspire (us) with

---

[70]   Philippians 1:6

desires which cannot be realized; so in spite of (our) littleness, (we) can hope to be a saint."[71]

---

[71]    St. Therese, *Story of a Soul, page 140*

# DAY 13

## ABRAHAM AND JOSEPH: KNOWN RATHER THAN NOTICED

> What then shall we say about Abraham, our forefather according to the flesh? For if Abraham was justified by works, he has something to boast about, but not before God. For what does scripture say? "Abraham believed God, and it was reckoned to him as righteousness." Now to one who works, his wages are not reckoned as a gift but as his due. And to one who does not work but trusts Him Who justifies the ungodly, his faith is reckoned as righteousness...We say that faith was reckoned to Abraham as righteousness.[72]

My friend, the man who believes that his works justify him in the sight of God is likely one who believes that his works must be noticed by others. He works to be noticed, hoping that others will affirm that he is noticed by God. Yet the man whose concern is for being noticed will not allow himself to be authentically known, for he is concerned with his works, that is, his appearance; and this appearance is guarded, that he may not be humiliated by becoming known for who he truly is.

Abraham did not make himself noticed by his works, but rather God made Abraham known, throughout the ages, because of his faith in God. The difference between making oneself noticed and being made known by God is the difference between performing works to appear righteous to God and being righteous before God because of one's faith in God.

---

[72] Romans 4:1; 5,9

Thus faith releases the human father from the shackles of the desire to be noticed, that is, from the attempt to earn favor with God by grasping at greatness. Faith empowers a father to believe that God will make him known, and make him great, primarily by means of his vocation as husband and father. Indeed, the reason we hail Abraham as our father of faith is because he believed that "he should become the father of many nations; as he had been told, 'So shall your descendants be.'" He did not weaken in faith when he considered his own body, which was as good as dead because he was about a hundred years old, or when he considered the barrenness of Sarah's womb. No distrust made him waver concerning the promise of God, but he grew strong in his faith as he gave glory to God, fully convinced that God was able to do what he had promised. That is why his faith was "reckoned to him as righteousness."[73]

Even though the vocation of fatherhood does not appear grand and lofty, and though it does not obtain the praises of the world, we too should believe like Abraham, having faith in God, glorifying God by being fully convinced that God's name can and will be glorified through our own personal vocation of fatherhood. My brother, one of the greatest temptations against the faith of a father is to believe that his hidden, unnoticed, humble fatherhood is not a sufficient vocational path, and therefore to attempt to "make a name"[74] for himself by means of other endeavors—even "Christian" endeavors—while neglecting the primary role and duty of fatherhood.

As with Abraham, the life of Joseph was very much unnoticed by others. Yet Joseph was made known by God because of his faith in God; a faith which granted him the role of being the father of the Son of God. This unnoticed father, virtually unknown in his day,

---

73    Romans 4:18-22
74    Reference to Tower of Babel - See Genesis 11

is today more known and lauded than any human father in history, and is heralded by the Church as "Joseph most faithful."[75]

When the Jews murmured in regards to Jesus' proclamation that He was the "Bread of Life," they protested, "Is not this Jesus, the son of Joseph, whose father and mother we know?"[76] And again, "Is not this the carpenter's son?"[77]

Initially, Jesus was known as the son of Joseph, but later and forever, Joseph became known in relationship to Jesus, as the man who spiritually adopted the Son of God. Joseph may once have been "known" by the Jews as Joseph the carpenter, but today Joseph is less known for his artisan skills than as the father of Jesus and the husband of the Mother of God.

My brother, in the end, you will not be known so much for your talents, gifts and occupational successes, as for how you fathered your children and loved your wife.

Both Abraham and Joseph were made known by God for their faith in the heir promised to each of them, and each of their heirs made their fatherhood known to the world. Good fathers assist in raising good children, and good children help to make their good fathers known.

Abraham and Joseph are known for their fatherhood, and you, my fellow father, if you respond to your vocation of fatherhood with faith like that of these two men, convinced that God will be glorified through what some may believe to be an all but dead vocation, will also be made known as a faithful father; "for nothing is hid that shall not be made manifest, nor anything secret that shall not be known."[78]

---

[75]   Litany to St. Joseph

[76]   John 6:42

[77]   Matthew 13:55

[78]   Luke 8:17

# DAY 14

Secrecy is the fatherly character that flows from the decision to be known to God alone. Without the decision to be known to God rather than noticed by men, a father cannot obtain this essential characteristic of fatherhood from God, and if he cannot obtain this character of secrecy from God, he will struggle, if not altogether fail, to become an icon of God the Father.

Indeed, our Lord, in His great sermon, revealed how fathers are to imitate God the Father. Three times within this powerful sermon Jesus focused upon the attribute of the heavenly Father's secrecy, while also commanding human fathers (and all people) to imitate such divine hiddenness:

> But when you give alms, do not let your left hand know what your right hand is doing, so that your alms may be given in secret; and your Father Who sees in secret, will reward you.[79]

> But when you pray, go into your room, and closing your door, pray to your Father in secret; and your Father, Who sees in secret will reward you.[80]

> But you, when you do fast, anoint your head and wash your face, so that you may not be seen fasting by men, but by your Father Who *is in secret*; and your Father Who sees in secret will reward you.[81]

---

[79] Matthew 6:3-4

[80] Matthew 6:6

[81] Matthew 6:17-18, emphasis added

Within the context of discussing the most basic Christian acts of almsgiving, prayer, and fasting, our Lord reveals that all of our actions should be motivated by the desire to perform these works for God alone, Who sees in secret, rather than for the glory and praise of men.

Our Lord also discloses that the reason for such secrecy is to imitate the "Father Who is in secret." God the Father lives in secret, moves in secret, and blesses in secret; for He is in secret. God the Father is a hidden, mysterious, and secret father, Who moves and works in hiddenness and silence without show or demonstration. God, our Father, does not put Himself on display, but rather reveals Himself to fathers who are willing to enter that secret place where He abides.

You, my fellow father, are to imitate this divine secrecy. In doing so, you will assist in directing the world toward God in heaven. This is a great paradox: the more secret your fatherhood becomes, the more the heavenly Father will be made known through your fatherhood. Indeed, on the father's part, this paradoxical truth demands great faith, but fear not, for this faith will be rewarded as was the faith of Abraham and Joseph. If, my brother, you choose to perform all of your life's actions with the motivation of being seen by your Father Who sees in secret, moves in secret, and blesses in secret, your Father Who is in secret will repay you.

Notice, my brother, that the vocation of fatherhood is a call to the silent, hidden, secret life; to the daily summons of tenderly rearing children, honoring a wife, and feeding a household with material and spiritual bread. A father's mission is to protect, feed, and teach his children in a secret manner, like that of God the Father toward His Son.

This "secret service" of self-sacrificial love will eventually, even perhaps for a prolonged period of time, remain unnoticed by the world, much like the tree that grows silently over time until, after many years have passed, people gaze in wonder at its achievement of such towering heights.

Be not afraid of being unnoticed, hidden, and secret. Your vocation of fatherhood is a refining fire that burns away the rust and impure accretions, that is, the disordered desires, primarily by means of the secret service which your vocation demands. Indeed, by asking for and receiving the gift of divine secrecy, you, my brother, will become humble, thus defeating pride and bringing glory to God, Who will one day glorify you.

While it is true that you ought to "let your light shine before men that they may see your good works and give glory to God,"[82] we must also keep in mind that light shines naturally, demonstrating that a source exists within the object, a source which produces the light. For example, the sun, as a planet of fire, produces light by the interior movements of molecules and gasses, all of which produce a brilliant light that shines, penetrating the darkness of the universe. Likewise, a father's work is accomplished in natural silence, producing a light that shines of its own accord and therefore needs no announcement.

Secrecy is not a defiant, tight-lipped rejection of others. This is contrary to the Word. Secrecy is way of life, wherein the father interiorizes all of his life and offers each moment to his Father in heaven as an act of secret homage, as an act of secret love. Just as the heavenly Father offers us His love in secret, silent, hidden ways, so too we offer Him our tokens of self-sacrifice, suffering, thanksgiving, and praise in the secret of our heart.

To offer the Father secret homage, a father refrains from boasting when he has accomplished a goal or fulfilled a task, and instead lifts his heart in thanksgiving to the God Who has blessed the work of his hands. The secret father refuses to grumble or complain about his work, his children, his wife, his own failings, or those of

---

[82]    Matthew 5:16

others, but rather he offers these sufferings and inconveniences to His heavenly father as an act of love. This is the secret way of fatherhood. This is the secret to becoming a faithful father.

All of these offerings, unknown to the world around him, occur in the interiority of the heart of the father who does these things in secret, and the Father Who sees in secret will indeed repay him.

# DAY 15

## The Secrecy of Abraham and Joseph

Both Abraham and Joseph are known today as men of faith, and each manifested his faith in responding to God's promise to him of an heir, a son. Both of these patriarchs are known because of their belief in God, and this belief became known through the testimony of their sons.

> When Abraham was tested by God to sacrifice his only son Isaac, "Abraham rose early in the morning, saddled his ass, and took two of his young men with him, and his son Isaac, and...on the third day Abraham lifted up his eyes and saw the place afar off. Then Abraham said to his young men, 'Stay here with the ass; I and the lad will go yonder and worship, and come again to you.'"[83]

Notice, my brother, that Abraham kept hidden, within the secrecy of his heart, the act which he was about to do. Abraham spoke nothing of his inner turmoil, heartache or pain at having to sacrifice his only son Isaac. Abraham did not mention to his hired hands that he would be sacrificing his son on mount Moriah. Rather, he kept the thoughts of the Lord within the secret of his heart. In fact, Abraham's "secrecy", that is, his ability to give his sufferings to God interiorly, is demonstrated in the fact that he spoke not a word to Isaac. Indeed, this is the key to secrecy: when you, my brother, offer sacrifice to the Lord, keep the sacrifice secret, between you and God, and God Who sees in secret will reward you.

---

[83]  Genesis 22:3, 5

The alms, the prayers, and the fasting of a father are those internal sufferings which are secretly sacrificed to God on behalf of the salvation of souls, particularly the souls of his own family members.

Abraham's silence and secrecy later became known by means of his grown son Isaac, who surely related this account to his children, and his children to their children's children. God also allowed the author of the letter of Hebrews to reveal even more of Abraham's interior thoughts, when he stated: "He considered that God was able to raise men even from the dead."[84]

Abraham lived a life of interior secrecy, offering himself to the Father, and God the Father made his secret faith known to the world.

My brother, let us also consider the secrecy of St. Joseph, who, like Abraham, received direction from God concerning his Son Jesus, not to sacrifice Him, but rather to save Him from Herod's murderous threat:

> "Rise, take the child and his mother, and flee to Egypt, and remain there till I tell you; for Herod is about to search for the child to destroy him." And he rose and took the child and his mother by night, and departed for Egypt.[85]

Like Abraham, Joseph did not reveal the divine message he received to the local villagers, neighbors or friends, but rather secretly fled from Bethlehem in the darkness of the night. This secret act, only known to Mary, was accomplished by the grace of God through Joseph, was made known by means of the life of his Son, Jesus. Joseph, the father of Jesus, secretly hid the Son, and the Son revealed the hidden secret of his human "foster" father.

Let us discover the secrets revealed in this hidden act. In this account, Joseph becomes the symbol of heroic fatherhood, that is,

---

[84]    Hebrews 11:19

[85]    Matthew 2:13-14

a father who defeats the malignant efforts of Satan, symbolized by Herod and his murderous envy. Joseph saves the child and the child's mother, escaping in the darkness of the night, symbolizing the secrecy of family life, the hidden, unknown ways of fatherhood, which are often unnoticed and hidden from the world.

You, my brother, like Joseph, have the responsibility to use your fatherhood to raise your family heroically, without pomp or self-glory: protecting, feeding and teaching them in the hiddenness of your family life, allowing your children to grow safe and hidden from the assailing evils of this world.

This by no means indicates that you are to remove your children from the world. Rather, this is a calling to protect, feed, and teach your children within the secret confines of the domestic church—the family life ordained by God—interiorly offering such sacrificial service to God in secret.

By means of both Abraham's and Joseph's example of secrecy, we discover that secrecy is the characteristic of a human father who offers internally all of his sufferings—not just alms, prayers, and fasting, but all actions, all sentiments, all joys, all sorrows, all miseries, all successes, and all failures—to the Father in the secret of his heart, unstained by the desire or motivation to be noticed by mankind.

To offer such acts of love and self-sacrifice to the Father without the desire or motivation to be noticed demands great faith and trust in the truth that the heavenly Father not only sees all, but also receives all. If you, my brother, integrate this divine characteristic of the Father's secrecy into your own fatherhood, offering all to Him Who has offered all to you, you will be living the Prayer of Faith, the foundation of a father's life of prayer.

*Obedience*

# DAY 16

The second component of the Prayer of Faith is obedience. Just as "faith without works is dead,"[86] so also listening without the action of obedience is useless; for what good is listening and receiving direction if that direction is not acted upon?

As stated previously, obedience has three main aspects. First, obedience is a proof of faith. If a man has faith in God, he will purposefully listen to God, and such listening presupposes that within the man there exists a certain level of willingness to act and submit himself to what he hears. To be obedient also presupposes that the father is subject to an authority greater than his own. By what authority does the father have authority, and to what authority is he subject? In other words, to what authority must the father be obedient in order to prove his faith? By engaging these questions we will arrive at a deeper understanding of obedience as a proof of faith.

The second aspect of fatherly obedience is demonstrated by a father's deliberate decision fully to reconcile with and dedicate himself to his wife and children. A father's commitment to remain submissive to God by continually receiving his wife in her entirety, while also receiving the offspring she bears to him, constitutes a portion of a father's proof of faith in God and the vocation God has granted him.

The third aspect of obedience is the sacrifice a father makes when his faith is tested. This type of sacrifice usually marks a

---

[86]  James 2:24

turning point in a man's life. The sacrifice may be as apparently small as removing a serious distraction, which up to this point has prevented the father from fulfilling his vocation with fervor and intention; or this sacrifice can be alarmingly substantial, causing tremendous pain, such as when a father accepts God's will upon losing a loved one, or permanently severs himself from his former lifestyle of sinful addictions and unhealthy relationships for the sake of God the Father, Christ, and His Gospel. Such trials are a preparation for the ultimate test of fatherhood: the choice to sacrifice one's own child by sacrificing one's selfish desires to prepare one's child for self-sacrifice.

Though "obedience is better than sacrifice,"[87] the act of obedience, per se, is an act of renouncing one's own will, one's own personal desires, and such renouncements are often mingled with deeply interior, personal sacrifices. When faced with this truth, the human father experiences a test of faith.

By comparing the obedience of Abraham with that of "Joseph most obedient,"[88] and studying the deep typological connection between our "father of faith" and the "faithful father" Joseph, we will, my brother, by God's grace, discover our own personal need for the gift of obedience and how necessary this gift is to the success of our own vocational efforts.

---

[87]   1 Samuel 15:22

[88]   Litany of St. Joseph

# DAY 17

After receiving the grace of guidance, which is a fruit of silently listening to God, a father must submit to the grace received. If a father chooses not to submit and obey such divine guidance, the opportunity to receive the associated particular graces may not be granted twice. Indeed, obedience is the other side of the listening coin. Listening and obedience are sister actions: listening makes obedience possible, and obedience proves that one has listened; both together prove that a man is faithful to God.

The words, "it is not sacrifice I desire but an open ear,"[89] demonstrate that God desires us to listen to His voice; and the words, "obedience is better than sacrifice,"[90] demonstrate that God desires us to be obedient. Listening and obedience work together harmoniously to fulfill God's holy will.

Indeed, "obedience is better than sacrifice,"[91] for obedience from the heart is the heart's humble sacrifice of all that is prideful. Truly, the fundamental characteristic of sacrifice is to be obedient to God's will, even and especially against those biting temptations that pressure one to gratify one's disordered passions, or the weaknesses of the spirit such as pride. All sacrifice is not an expression of obedience, but only the sacrifice offered from the heart, in an effort to follow God's will obediently, is true sacrifice.

---

[89]   Psalm 40:6
[90]   1 Samuel 15:22
[91]   ibid

My brother, to be obedient to the holy will of God, we must exercise great faith, believing that God has already granted the necessary grace to fulfill His will. Indeed He has! It is more important that we obey in faith, than that we accomplish the good work we believe we are called to complete. God is more interested in the heart's willingness to surrender obediently to His will than in any accomplishment or great work.

The difference between submitting obediently to what God asks of us and accomplishing something which God did not request is the difference between being justified by God or attempting to justify ourselves. Only the man of faith who obeys the will of God will be justified; for the Lord said, "Not everyone who says to Me, 'Lord, Lord,' shall enter the kingdom of heaven, but he who does the will of My Father in heaven." The words of Jesus continue,

> Many will say to Me in that day, "Lord, Lord, have we not prophesied in Your name, cast out demons in Your name, and done many wonders in Your name?" And then I will declare to them, "I never knew you; depart from Me, you who practice lawlessness." [92]

From our Lord's words we discover that a man cannot justify himself by his own works, but rather he is justified by God—by faith which inspires him to do God's will obediently.

It may sound paradoxical to say that one is justified by faith in God, but that one's faith demands an associated good work of obedience. Yet the good work per se cannot justify any man; rather, God justifies a man whose faith is strong enough to produce obedience. For this reason, a man is justified by faithfully obeying God rather than trusting in his own efforts; for one who trusts in the Lord, obeying God's command, yet fails to accomplish the task at hand, has accomplished more than the man who does not obey in faith and yet apparently accomplishes much. The true

---

[92]    Matthew 7:21

accomplishment is not in the outward results but in obeying the Lord's will.

God the Father can accomplish more with the obedient acts of a father who, in the secret of his heart, offers such failures with obedience, than with a man's apparently successful actions. When God calls you, my brother, to obey His will faithfully, believe with faith, and that faith will activate the already-given grace, enabling you to fulfill His command obediently. Remember, my brother, that the grace is already given, and that you need only the faith to access it.

It is also important to understand that disobedience, in its deepest essence, is a lack of faith in the generosity of God. When a heart becomes disobedient, it removes its trust from God, while placing its hope in something else, which then becomes its god.

Faith in God and His generosity inspires one to obey, and obedience proves one's faith. "To obey (from the Latin ob-audire, to 'hear or listen to') in faith is to submit freely to the word that has been heard because its truth is guaranteed by God, Who is Truth itself."[93]

Indeed, a deep bond exists between obedience and listening, which if broken can rupture the destiny of the soul, particularly the soul of a father. My brother, we are to embrace silence in prayer, and in silence we are to listen, and by listening we will receive promptings from God, which will guide and direct our lives, unveiling our failings and sins, shedding light on what needs to be corrected, awakening holy desires, providing insights, drawing us into the heavens—into a deep and abiding communion with the Triune God.

After the listening heart of a father has discerned God's direction, he must "submit freely to the word that has been heard,"[94] responding courageously with a calm determination to follow obediently the divine direction that he has received.

---

[93] CCC 144
[94] ibid

If a father believes he has received direction from God, he should follow such promptings with strict obedience lest he neglect the gift God desires to grant to him. Even if a father errs by obeying such promptings, believing them to be of divine origin when they are not, God knows and sees the sincerity of the human heart, knowing that the father's willingness to obey is authentic, He will assist His child, offering future opportunities of obedience and helping him hear God's voice more clearly. Just as a human father will not condemn a child who longs to obey and yet misunderstands the direction given, but will rather patiently explain his directions in more detail, so too it is with God giving direction to His children. This does not mean that a father is to neglect the process of discernment. Rather, this process, combined with means which we will discuss in the Prayer of Meditation, will enable him more accurately to perceive when it is the Lord speaking and when it is another.

Whom does a father obey? Who has authority over the human father?

The saints and holy doctors explain that if a person desires to be sanctified he must be obedient to his superior, regardless of how trivial the matter may appear. The parish priest, for example, is to be obedient to his Bishop, the Bishop is to be obedient to the Pope, the cloistered brother to his Abbot, the sister to her superior, children to their parents, wives to their husbands.[95] To whom should the human father submit his authority?

Within the context of the family, the father is the patriarch, the person vested with authority as priest and king over his domestic sanctuary. Indeed, within the hierarchy of the family, there is no greater authority than that of a father. "Wives are to be subject to (their) husbands, as is fitting in the Lord. Husbands (should) love

---

[95]   1 Peter 3:1

(their) wives and not be harsh with them. Children (are to) obey (their) parents in everything, for this pleases the Lord."[96]

From these scriptures we obtain a clear vision of the hierarchal order of the family: children are to submit in obedience to parents, and a wife is to submit to the authority of her husband. Yet the question remains: to whom must a father submit his authority?

To receive authority presupposes that another has granted that authority. If one expects obedience to one's authority, one must be obedient to the source of that authority. The human father's hierarchal position is unique within the order of creation. As to faith and morals the father is under the authority of the Church, but as to the daily governance of his household, the Church bears witness that the human father receives his authority from God alone.[97] It is to this divine authority that the father must submit.

This position of authority, within the context of the family, situates the father in a spiritually open space, a vast frontier, a world of both great freedom and tremendous responsibility, wherein he stands between the family and God's throne. Because of this, a father can misunderstand such liberty as a freedom to serve himself, his passions, and his boyish dreams. The human father could easily misinterpret this position between God and his family as "his space," "his frontier," and "his freedom" to do as he pleases.

In truth, however, this position of authority is accompanied by the heavy demand that a father respond fully and continually to God's command to serve his wife and children. The frontier is vast, allowing a father the freedom to determine as best he can how to serve his family—but serve them he must, if he is to remain faithful to the source of his freedom and authority.

The human father's unique hierarchal position is one of tremendous responsibility, for the authority he has received from God

---

[96] See Colossians 3: 18-21

[97] See Genesis chapter 2 and Ephesians chapter 5

the Father he must use to father his family in imitation of the divine model. If he expects obedience from his children and submission from his wife, the human father must obey and submit to God and His direction.

You, my fellow father, are to establish, within your family, the pattern for obedience and service. If you are obedient to the divine model, the Bridegroom Jesus Christ, Who established the pace for self-giving love for his bride the Church, then and only then will you be able to set the pace for self-giving love in your family.

# DAY 18

## ABRAHAM AND JOSEPH:
### FAITH PROVEN BY OBEDIENCE

By faith, Abraham obeyed when he was called to go out to a place which he was to receive as an inheritance, and he went out "not knowing where to go." By faith, he lived as a stranger and pilgrim in the Promised Land. By faith, Sarah was given to conceive of the promise. And by faith Abraham offered his only son in sacrifice.[98]

My brother, within this brief summary of Abraham's faith we discover four ways in which he obeyed the Lord's direction, thus proving his faith in God: first, Abraham went out not knowing where to go; second, Abraham lived as a stranger in a foreign land; third, Abraham trusted that his wife would conceive and bear him a son; and fourth, Abraham offered his only son in sacrifice.

Abraham's four faith-filled acts of obedience are also typologically correlated to Joseph, who first trusted that his wife Mary would conceive and bear a Son; second, was directed by the Lord in a dream to go to Egypt, a land he did not know; third, lived as a stranger in a foreign land; and fourth, by means of preparation and loving self-sacrifice, prepared his Son to offer Himself as the ultimate sacrifice on behalf of sinners.

These four acts of obedience, demonstrating the faith of Abraham and Joseph, constitute a four-fold proof of faith for all fathers.

---

[98]    CCC 145

The first two proofs of faith, setting out without knowing where to go, and living as a stranger in a foreign land, fall within this mark of obedience, "Obedience as a Proof of Faith." The third proof of faith, which is receiving the promised offspring that a wife gives, will comprise the next mark of obedience, "Embracing One's Vocation as Husband and Father." The last proof of faith, the sacrifice of one's own child, pertains to the last mark of obedience, "Test of Faith."

By faith Abraham obeyed the Lord's command to "Go from your country and your kindred and your father's house to the land I will show you."[99] "So, Abram went as the Lord had told him,"[100] and "he went out not knowing where to go."[101]

Joseph, also by faith, obeyed the Lord's command to "rise, take the child and his mother, and flee to Egypt";[102] "and so he rose by night, and departed to Egypt,"[103] not knowing where to go.

My brother, notice how both Abraham and Joseph, by means of their listening hearts, were receptive to the divine direction given to them. This divine guidance, however, did not fully reveal the destination of either of their journeys; only that they should journey, even if they did "not know the way to go." Like these two exemplars of fatherhood, you also, my brother, if you listen carefully, will discern your call to embark upon the true journey of fatherhood without knowing the ultimate outcome, without comprehending how your story will end. Nevertheless, you must set out, even if you do not know the way. Even if you have been a father for years, and yet realize you have not truly fathered your children, it is never too late to respond to the call to set out on this journey of true fatherhood.

---

99    Genesis 12:1
100   Genesis 12:4
101   Hebrews 11:8
102   Matthew 2:13
103   Matthew 2:14

This is the path of every young father who begins the journey, the adventure of fatherhood, which he embraces with little knowledge or experience, but only the call to father in God's image. Like Abraham knowing he was to depart for the Promised Land, or Joseph knowing he was to depart for Egypt, we know that we are ultimately to image the Fatherhood of God to this world, and yet we do not know the way.

Indeed, you do not know how many children your wife will give you, or how many years of life God will grant to you, or what will become of your children, or how you will provide for your family, or what demands and obstacles will arise in pursuit of fulfilling this grand vocational mission. In fact, a father only ever knows that he knows not the way, and yet that he has been called to this fatherly way of faith.

Many men embark upon the mission of fatherhood either by mistake or accident; others approach it with an airy idealism; still others approach it with faith in God. Only the last will succeed in their efforts to complete the journey. The first proof of a father's faith in the Father of heaven is accepting the call and committing himself to being a great father, knowing that he knows not the way. If, at the onset of his vocational mission, God showed a father all that would be demanded and how it would end, many fathers, if not most, would not undertake the challenge for fear of failure, or from an unwillingness to sacrifice themselves for their children.

God calls us to fatherhood, and yet we know not the way to ideal fatherhood, or rather, to becoming the father God is calling each of us to be. We cannot control our future or our destiny; God alone knows the way of our fatherhood. Yet we do know that, wherever God is calling us individually, this way is an imitation of Joseph's way: the way of fatherly greatness. It is better, my brother, that you do not "know the way," but rather respond each day to the call of fatherhood laid before you, and by doing this prove your faith, as did Abraham and Joseph before you.

The second proof of faith is "living as a stranger" in a foreign land.[104] If you, my brother, are committed to responding to the call of fatherhood, you will become like Abraham and Joseph, that is, a stranger in your own land. Indeed, by responding faithfully to the duty and mission of leading and serving your family, you will quickly realize the alarming level of evil which has saturated the world around you. All that is necessary for a man to recognize the evil around him is to see the world through his child's innocent eyes. While encountering the reality of a world dominated by the evil one, who is bent on deceiving and destroying your children—for the devil's desire is to "devour the child"[105]—you will be faced with twin temptations.

On one side, you will be tempted to minimize the powers of the evil one and his influence upon the world, naively believing that your child will be exempt from harmful influences, or persuading yourself that the harmful influences are not so harmful at all. By submitting to this temptation, the human father has already surrendered in the battle to assist his child in becoming another Christ.

On the other side, you will be tempted to remove yourself and your children from the world, attempting to isolate your family from all harmful influences. This too, is a grave mistake; for by removing yourself and your family from the world, you seem to be denying the good of God in his creation, while also potentially instilling a deep-seated suspicion of all men, thus leading your child to commit the sin of judging others instead of loving them.

Another harm in removing one's family from the world is the missed opportunity of preparing your children to inject themselves and their Christian faith into this needy world. Indeed, we fathers and our families must live in the world, but not be of the world.

The father of faith, like Abraham our "father in faith" and "Joseph most faithful," ought to live with his family amidst the

---

[104]   See Genesis 23:4 and Matthew 2:14
[105]   See Revelation 12

world, obeying God by living as a stranger in a foreign land, while also preparing his children to offer themselves to God as a thanksgiving offering.

It is also significant, my brother, that Abraham "By faith, lived as a stranger and pilgrim in the Promised Land."[106] Abraham lived as a stranger, as a pilgrim, in the Promised Land as an example to all fathers who, not knowing the way to go, are also pilgrims in the promised land of their very vocation. Both Abraham and Joseph lived in the promised land of their own vocation of fatherhood, living in the fulfilled promises of the Lord, living amongst their own families, their own promised heirs, bearing their God-given authority as "lord of [their] household(s) and prince(s) over all [their] possessions."[107] In this land of promise they existed in a fatherly solitude, standing in the vulnerability of the unknown, unforeseeable, uncertain future.

Indeed, the human father, within his own family, experiences the promised blessings of communal love, while also and simultaneously experiencing the internal ache of being a stranger among them, whose responsibility to protect, to feed and to teach his family, in some sense, differentiates him from his family in his unique position before God. From this position he must lead the way to the promised, eternal Fatherland by means of his obedient, faith-filled response to God.

---

[106] CCC 145
[107] Litany of St. Joseph

# DAY 19

### Abraham's and Joseph's God-Given Authority

Now that we have examined both Abraham and Joseph and their deep typological connection with regards to obedience, it is also fitting that we briefly examine their unique position of fatherly authority within the family, and how this position of authority is subject to the heavenly Father's authority.

Both Abraham and Joseph, in regards to their vocation, received direction directly from God. This direction granted each of them authority to direct their families in fulfilling the holy will of God. Indeed, God the Father, the ultimate Authority, grants fathers the ability to transmit the Word to the members of their own families. Without this inspired understanding, a father often misuses his authority, becoming tyrannical or self-seeking, undermining his true God-given responsibility.

As stated previously, a father is under no earthly authority regarding the governance of his family. This paradigm of fatherly authority, as revealed by Sacred Scripture, was established by God from the beginning, with Abraham, our "father in faith," and re-confirmed with the father, "Joseph most faithful." Both of these fathers received direction from the Lord, Who established the human father as patriarch over his family.

Though the father is directed by God to lead his family to holiness, this does not indicate that he is not accountable for his actions toward his wife and children. Indeed, the father demonstrates his authority by submitting to God's authority, and by submitting to God, His Word, His Church, and His inspirations, the father, in all humility, should never oppose that which is from God in his family members.

For example, when a father commits a sin and is corrected by his wife or children, he is to subject himself to God speaking to him through his wife or children. Though such direction may appear to have come from his subjects, the father, by being obedient to the divine law of love, is in fact subjecting himself to the direction of his heavenly Father.[108] Likewise, in his righteous actions the father is to live to serve and uphold the dignity of his family, expecting them to obey him only after he has set the example of righteousness.

By exercising such obedience, the father proves his faithfulness to the authority of God and thus legitimates his God-given authority. You also, my brother, ought to follow the obedient example of Abraham and Joseph by being obedient to the authority of God, and by accepting your God-given authority. At times you may have to admonish your subjects, while on other occasions you may have to accept their fraternal correction as God's own direction and correction for your soul. Humility coupled with faith will prove your obedience, and being obedient you will prove your faith.

---

[108]  See Genesis 21: Sarah tells Abraham to send out the slave women Hagar, and God directs Abraham to obey her. This indicates that God is the one directing, not Sarah per se, though in this case God chose to direct Abraham through Sarah.

# DAY 20

## THE SECOND ASPECT OF OBEDIENCE:
## RECEPTIVITY TO ONE'S WIFE AND OFFSPRING

As stated previously, the second aspect of fatherly obedience is demonstrated by a father's deliberate decision to dedicate himself to his wife and children. This fatherly commitment is a continual re-dedication of himself to serve his wife and children as Christ served and loved the Church.

Remember that you, my fellow father, are to establish within your family the pattern of obedience and service. If you are obedient to the divine model, the Bridegroom Jesus Christ, the definitive revelation of God, Who established the pace for self-giving love for his bride the Church, then you will be better able to set the pace for self-giving love in your family.

Though this message is particularly focused upon fatherhood, its essential role in the economy of salvation, and the effect it has upon the ultimate destiny of the world, it is also important to examine briefly the essential role and vocation of the husband, for without the powerful Sacrament of Marriage, our children, from the onset, are hindered in achieving the goal of becoming holy and living sacrifices to the Lord.

My brother, the best gift you can give your children is a good, holy, faithful marriage. Strong adults commonly begin as strong children, and strong children come from strong marriages. If your children have the gift and opportunity to live under the canopy of a harmonious, self-giving, faithful marriage, they will be better equipped to become virtuous, faith-filled, self-giving adults.

To best ensure that you are providing your children with a strong marital example, you and your wife must strive to become a united front, a harmonious integration of persons, appearing as one before your children. The united front between a husband and wife is the key component to raising children to become virtuous, self-giving, honorable individuals. If you, my brother, desire to have a holy family, you should pay particular attention to striving to become one with your wife.

There are multiple factors to consider when striving to unify a marriage, but for our purposes we will focus only upon the husband's most basic and primary responsibilities in relationship to his wife. Again, because of personality types, culture, individual needs, and other factors, a multitude of variables should be considered when striving to unite yourself more fully with your bride. Still, there exist three fundamental aspects of being a good husband, which should always be considered as foundational.

First, a husband must understand his essence, that is, the fundamental meaning of being a man, which always entails being a husband who lives in relationship with his wife. Whether a celibate priest or a husband engaging his sexual faculties, a man is one who lives in relationship with his bride. Once a man has knowledge of the ontological truth of his being, he is more capable of understanding and fulfilling his mission as both husband and father.

Second, a husband who sincerely desires to fulfill this mission should imitate the perfect Bridegroom, Jesus Christ, by loving his bride in the manner Christ loves His. To follow such an example indicates that the husband must study and learn from the example of Christ in relationship to His bride the Church. Christ's example of fidelity to, and self-giving love for, His bride, helps a husband to keep check on the many temptations to become domineering or to dismiss himself from ongoing and continual service to his family. The husband who follows the command of Christ, "learn from me,"[109] will be continually refortified and refreshed with Christ's living water, which will enable him to love his bride.

Third, a husband should strive by means of prayer, self-denial, and humility to defeat lust in his heart. Lust is a cancer which is bent on corrupting every man's heart. Indeed, lust is especially a male problem, a deeply rooted weed in the garden of love, which, if not attacked, will become a thicket of thorns causing much pain to both the husband and his wife. The battle against lust is among the most fundamental issues for the husband, and if not properly dealt with, this malignant force will undermine, if not destroy altogether, his hope for building the domestic church.

Although factors such as communication, spousal responsibilities, intimacy, finances, and child rearing are important and must be continually addressed, all of these factors depend upon the three foundational aspects of being a virtuous husband: first, knowing the essence and core character of a man; second, following the example of Christ, the divine Bridegroom; and third, maintaining purity of heart and fighting the tenacious interior battle to overcome and eventually, by God's grace, defeat lust.

By examining these aspects of being a virtuous husband through the lens of Abraham and Joseph we will more readily understand the meaning of being a holy husband, enabling us to press on to discuss what it means to receive the offspring our wives so generously bear.

---

[109]  Matthew 11:29

# DAY 21

## The Essential Role of a Husband

My brother, your family will become unified to the degree that your marriage is unified, and your marriage will be unified by uniting your marriage to that of Christ and His Church. To offer that united, integrated front of harmonious marital and parental love to your children, you must understand your essential role and dignity as a man, a dignity that is discovered in the analogy of the marriage of Christ and His Church.

The author of Ephesians, speaking of this great marital analogy, calls all husbands, within their marriage, to establish the pace of self-giving love: "Be yourselves subject to one another. Wives be subject to husbands as to the Lord, for the husband is the head of the wife as Christ is the head of the Church, His body, and is Himself its Savior. As the Church is subject to Christ, so let wives also be subject in everything to their husbands. Husbands, love your wives, as Christ loved the Church and gave Himself up for her, that he might sanctify her." [110]

The man (or husband) in this analogy images Christ and His love for His Bride the Church. Christ's love for His Bride is a radical love, void of selfish motives, attentive to the continual building up of His Bride, even, if needed, at the expense of self. Union with God is the ultimate destiny for every husband, and this union between God and man is achieved when God's grace enables a man to die to self so that he may live in union with his bride.

---

[110] Ephesians 5:21-26

If the mystery of the relationship between God and man is in some way revealed by the marital analogy, then the mystery of man and his identity is also revealed by means of this analogy.

A man, in his essence, is a partner of the Absolute, a person who should strive, by God's grace, to become absolutely free of self-ishness by becoming fully self-giving, fully free. This union with God is accomplished primarily, in a husband, by means of his relationship to his bride, who is a symbol of the Bride of Christ, the Church.

This marital analogy demonstrates a common likeness between the husband and wife in that they are both destined for union with God. However, the martial analogy expresses a fundamental and essential difference between the husband and wife.

What then essentially differentiates a man from a woman? Man, like woman, is comprised of both body and soul; yet if the body expresses the deeper ontological reality of the human person, a man's body expresses that he is fundamentally and ontologically different than the woman. A man's body expresses the deep, interior reality that even though he is comprised of the same substance (body and soul) as the woman, this substance has a different character in him than it does in her.

Both men and women are created to give themselves away to another; however, a fundamental difference in the manner by which a man and woman fulfill this self-donation is apparent in their sexual difference. Man, taken in relation to woman, appears to be given the responsibility of setting the standard for the dynamic of self-giving love within the context of his marriage. The man is to establish the pace for the couple's growth in mutual self-donation, and is principally, although not solely, responsible for the progress of this loving union.

Today, some women resist the idea that a husband establishes the pace for self-giving love within the marriage, believing that they should also set the pace, or even dictate the standard for self-giving love. In part, this is due to men failing to initiate self-giving love, shrinking from their responsibility to sacrifice for the woman, and consequently tempting women to manipulate and coerce men into self-donation.

This failure on the part of men is itself partly a consequence of original sin, and it represents a falling away from fidelity to the distinct essences of man and woman. This dynamic originated with Adam and Eve, when Adam neglected to protect the woman. Eve, tempted by the serpent, and finding Adam unwilling to intervene self-sacrificially on her behalf, resorted to turning the temptation on him, manipulating her husband into responding to her, though in an impure fashion.

Indeed, two of the most notable examples of man's responsibility to set the standard of self-giving love within the context of the marital analogy are Adam, the first of all men, and the New Adam, Jesus Christ, the first-born of all men destined to be reborn.

The first Adam was given responsibility to "till and keep" the garden,[111] that is, "to guard and have charge of" of the garden. The word "garden," used often in the Sacred Scriptures, has both a literal and symbolic sense. The literal Garden of Eden was a symbol of the woman's garden, that is her interior subjective realm, her interior person, her purity and innocence. Adam was entrusted with the task of guarding and cherishing the garden of Eve.

When the serpent tempted the woman to eat of the fruit, which would defile her interior person, Adam neglected his responsibility to defend his bride, and rather allowed the serpent to have his way with Eve. Adam's lack of responsibility for the garden of Eve resulted in sin, shame, blame, and the disruption of harmony between body and soul, and sowed the seeds for continual ruptured relationships between the sexes through the ages.

---

[111]  See Genesis 2:15-21

Jesus, the New Adam, entering the garden on the night of His betrayal, rather than attempting to flee from the tremendous sufferings He faced, handed Himself over to His enemy, accepting responsibility for His Bride, that is, all of humanity, allowing her to escape the wrath that He endured on her behalf.

Jesus, the true man, submitted Himself completely to His Father, making Himself completely vulnerable, consequently bringing forth the union of the Bridegroom, that is, Jesus, and the Bride, that is, the Church, through His self-donation.

Both Adam and the New Adam established the pace for the dynamism of love, or absence thereof. The former established the paradigm of neglect, selfishness, and lust, while the latter set the paradigm of responsibility, of self-giving love, of complete self-donation.

By studying and comparing these two examples we discover the deepest ontological truth of man: man is essentially programmed to sacrifice himself on behalf of his bride. Without the experience at some level of such self-sacrifice on behalf of God, in union with Christ, and given freely for his wife, a husband has not achieved manhood, nor is he fully alive.

The Sacrament of marriage was created by God to be one of the most powerfully expressive, undeniably purifying, and radically self-giving models of Christian love. Indeed, marriage is highly purgative in character. Two people, of opposite sex, commit themselves as husband and wife to live as two distinct persons, yet also as one flesh, one person, by freely choosing radical selflessness for the sake of the other. The fruit of marriage, which is the family, is the primary context in which husbands, wives, and children are to grow and be purified in the fire of radical self-giving love.

God the Father, Who has expressed Himself fully in the person of Jesus Christ, has granted every father authority to image God's Fatherhood by doing what Jesus did, that is, by serving his bride "so that she may have life and have it more abundantly."[112] Indeed, to father in God's image we must "husband" in Christ's image. By uniting ourselves to our bride as Christ unites Himself to His Church, we will become capable of fathering the domestic church.

-

---

[112]  John 10:10

# DAY 22

## A Husband's Practical Love

Let us, my brother, return to these words: "Husbands love your wives, just as Christ also loved the Church and delivered himself up for her."[113] And also, "A husband is head of the wife, just as Christ is head of the Church, being himself savior of the body."[114]

These scripture verses identify the husband as a symbol of Christ, while also commanding him to an order of love which demands of him that he be both lover and savior of his wife by means of the supernatural love of Christ afforded by the gift of grace.

This scripture also indicates that the wife operates as the body of the head, who is the husband; and that the husband should exceedingly love his body, honoring and glorifying it. As the author of Ephesians states: "he who loves his own wife, loves himself. For no one ever hated his own flesh; on the contrary he nourishes it and cherishes it, as Christ also does the Church."[115]

The husband's divinely ordained leadership over the common project of achieving full and complete integration in marriage is to be animated by the Spirit of the Savior Jesus Christ, Who inspires the husband to strive to become fully one with his bride, caring for her as though she is an integral part of his very person. As Pope John Paul II states:

---

[113] Ephesians 5:25

[114] Ephesians 5:23

[115] Ephesians 5:29

"Man becomes the image of God not so much in the moment of solitude as in the moment of communion...This constitutes, perhaps, the deepest theological aspect of all that can be said about man." [116] The "first man and the first woman must constitute the beginning and the model of the communion for all men and women who, in any period, are united so intimately as to be 'one flesh.'"[117] Masculinity and femininity, the wife and the husband, "complete each other."[118]

By creating man and woman for marriage and revealing to us the "great analogy" in the fifth chapter of the letter to the Ephesians, God demonstrates His desire to be one with us, and his desire that the covenant of marriage be an icon of this "great mystery" of Christ and His Church. Indeed, one of our Lord's last prayers preceding His passion was this:

> The glory that thou hast given me, I have given them; that they may
> be one, as we also are one: I in them, and thou in me; that they may
> be perfected in unity, and that the world may know that thou hast
> sent me, and that thou hast loved them even as thou hast loved me.[119]

The love of God unites and integrates a husband and wife so that they become a complete communion of persons, a living icon of Christ and His Church. By bearing fruit, both physically and spiritually, their spousal love can actually image the Trinity. This is accomplished when God gives His glory to the husband, who in turn gives himself without reserve to his wife, who is then inspired to reciprocate this self- giving love. Thus the wife returns the glory she has received from her husband to her husband, and therefore to God, Who is glorified by the union of husband and wife as they

---

[116]   Pope John Paul II, *Theology of the Body*, 46

[117]   Pope John Paul II, *Theology of the Body*, 50

[118]   Pope John Paul II, *Theology of the Body*, 48

[119]   John 17:22-23

more evidently become an icon of the mystical marriage of Christ and His Church.

As head of his wife, the husband who "delivers himself up for her"[120] fosters the dynamic of the gift, encouraging his wife to become the glorified person God has ordained her to be. By giving himself to her, and thus inspiring her gift of self in return, the husband sanctifies his wife.

Therefore a husband acts as Christ by granting his wife the glory which he himself has been given, striving with all his God-given energies, strengths, talents, and resources to die to himself continually that he may be integrated with her, glorifying the One Trinitarian God. Indeed, my brother, it is imperative that you pass on the glory, authority, and grace which you have received from God to your wife, so that the two of you can become a harmonious example of self-giving love to your children.

---

[120] Ephesians 5:25

# DAY 23

## The Husband Learns from Christ

"Take my yoke upon you, and learn from me, for I am meek and humble of heart; and you will find rest for your souls."[121]

Our Lord commands all people to learn from Him, and this command is particularly important for husbands within the context of marriage. Our Lord calls every husband to learn from His words, His example, His sacrifices, His passion, His self-giving love, which compelled Him to become completely vulnerable in order to give Himself on behalf of His bride.

Our Lord also encourages each and every husband to take His yoke upon him. A yoke was a constraint which locked around the neck of a beast of burden, with several ropes or cords which attached the yoke to a load, or burden. The beast of burden pulled the load by means of the yoke around its neck. When two oxen pulled the load, they would not simply pull double the weight, but because of a synergy between the beasts, they could pull a substantial amount more than the sum of what the two beasts were capable of pulling individually.

This dynamic holds true with Christ's yoke. Christ yokes Himself in two manners. First, Christ yokes Himself to His bride the Church, and the two become one in pulling the load of working out the salvation of mankind. Second, our Lord yokes Himself to husbands in that He commands each husband to love his wife as He has loved the Church. Christ calls every husband to partake in

---

[121]    Matthew 11:29

His mission of loving the Church by loving His very own bride and "delivering himself up for her."[122] If a husband delivers himself up for his bride, he is more likely to win over his wife, and being won over, his wife will join him in self-giving love, and they will become an icon of the marriage of Christ and His Church, glorifying the Living God as one flesh.

Such a task is impossible for a husband who is not animated by the Holy Spirit or is not responding to the redemptive grace necessary to die to his passions, particularly his pride and ego, which tempt him to believe himself superior to his wife. Yet to image and glorify God a husband and wife must "do nothing out of contentiousness or out of vainglory. But in humility...[each must] regard the other as his superior, each one not looking to his own interests but to those of others."[123]

When a husband takes on the yoke of Christ, he becomes strengthened, capable of carrying the load of marriage, dying to himself for his bride, and delivering himself up for her. This is because he is assisted by Christ Who animates him, enabling him to become meek and humble of heart.

A husband, strengthened by the Lord to Whom he is yoked, eventually finds rest and peace in his soul, in his marriage, and in his relationship with his wife; for the burden he carries "is easy and light."[124] It is Christ Who makes the burden of drawing the bride toward salvation easy and light. In other words, Christ makes loving our wives, glorifying our wives, dying to our pride for the sake of our wives, a delight which grants rest and peace to our souls.

---

[122]   Ephesians 5:25
[123]   Philippians 2:3
[124]   Matthew 11:30

# DAY 24

## THE EXAMPLE OF CHRIST: A PEDAGOGY FOR HUSBANDS

A husband yokes himself to his Lord's yoke, takes it upon himself, learning from the Master Who yoked Himself to humanity. By yoking himself to his Lord, he submits himself to being trained by Christ, Who teaches each husband how to love his wife, how to glorify her and deliver himself up for her. How does Christ teach this to husbands?

Male headship has been generally typified by two extremes. The ancient pagan model of headship, which often influenced Christian cultures, was traditionally characterized by the husband laying down rules or laws and imposing them upon his wife and children, whereas the modern model attempts to escape such male domination by means of feminism, a female domination which places the husband in a submissive role under the headship of his wife.

Neither of these types of headship have the character of charitable authority as exemplified and taught by Jesus Christ. Husbands can learn to love like Christ by studying His love for His Bride the Church, Whom He acknowledges as His own body. This is important, for the husband who is yoked to Christ, Who considers the Church His body, must also yoke himself to his wife and consider her as his own body. "Even thus ought husbands also to love their wives as their own bodies. He who loves his own wife, loves himself. For no one ever hated his own flesh; on the contrary he nourishes and cherishes it, as Christ also does the Church." [125]

Our Lord teaches every husband that he cannot command his wife and children to fulfill God's law, that is, the moral law of love, if he himself is not striving to fulfill God's law and offering his own self-sacrifice. Only a husband who is subject to God's moral law can expect his wife and family to fulfill the same law of love; for this is the example of Christ: He fulfilled the law of God perfectly, and therefore could expect his Bride to follow His holy example.

He says, "Do not think that I have come to destroy the Law or the Prophets. I have not come to destroy, but to fulfill."[126] And again we are told,

> Son though He was, He learned obedience from the things that he suffered; and when perfected, he became to all who obey him the cause of eternal life.[127] Wherefore it was right that he should in all things be made likened unto his brethren, that he might become merciful... For in that He Himself has suffered and has been tempted, He is able to help those who are tempted. [128]

Together, these three inspired texts comprise a rule or an example according to which husbands should measure the manner in which they exercise charitable authority over their wives. The three components of this rule of headship are: first, a personal striving to fulfill God's law of love; second, the learning of obedience through suffering; and third, the ability to grant mercy to one's wife because one understands the difficulty in overcoming temptation in the pursuit of fulfilling God's law.

God the Word, in His divine nature, was not capable of suffering, but by becoming incarnate, He obtained the power to perfect

---

[125] Ephesians 5:28-29
[126] Matthew 5:17
[127] Hebrews 5:8
[128] Hebrews 2:17-18

human nature by means of obeying the law of self-giving love, even to the point of profound and unspeakable sufferings. Though He is perfectly divine, Christ's human nature developed in wisdom and progressed in obedience, perfecting human nature through suffering, and therefore Christ is able to pass on the fruits of obedience— that is, redemptive grace—to His body the Church.

Our Lord was tempted in every way that His Bride would be tempted so that He might experience in his humanity the mercy needed by human beings who are crushed under temptation. Indeed, Christ became like us in everything but sin, becoming capable of imparting to us everything we need to become like Him.

Because He fulfilled the law Christ is able to give the grace to fulfill the same law, and in fact is able to grant this grace mercifully, understanding the difficulty demanded in overcoming such temptation.

Because Christ obediently fulfilled the law which he enjoined upon His bride, He can say, "Therefore all that you wish men to do to you, even so do you also to them; for this is the Law and the Prophets."[129] Within this context, these words can mean, "do not expect your wife to fulfill the moral law if you are not striving to fulfill it yourself." A husband cannot lead without following the law of God; for if he cannot learn to abide by God's law of love, how can he, as a husband, expect to impart the necessary grace for his wife to obey the moral law?

The One Who fulfilled the moral law imposes no law of morality upon His Bride which He Himself did not fulfill. For this reason He calls each and every husband, within the context of his marital relationship, to do to his wife as the husband also desires to be done to him; for this is the fulfillment of the Law.[130]

---

[129] Matthew 7:12

[130] The very next passage in scripture is the entry through the narrow gate. The path which Christ sets for husbands is indeed a narrow path, rather than the wide, smooth path of domination.

A husband who imposes the moral law upon his wife and not upon himself is removing the yoke of Christ, and designing a plan for salvation other than the Way Christ has given.

If the husband attempts to impose God's moral law upon his wife while not abiding with it himself, he undermines his very own headship, and rather than receiving the grace to fulfill the moral law, he is condemned by the law. My brother, consider Our Lord's judgment on such an action: "Do not judge, that you may not be judged. For with what judgment you judge, you shall be judged; and with what measure you measure, it shall be measured to you."[131] The husband who measures his bride by a law by which he does not measure himself subjects himself to the measure and judgment of God. "It is a fearful thing to fall into the hands of the living God."[132]

However, a husband who lives obediently by God's law of love, and is trained under the same law which he proposes to his family, learns the difficulty demanded in overcoming the temptation not to fulfill the law. Experiencing this tension and difficulty, he acts mercifully to his wife, who is striving to obey the same law.

Being trained under the same law as his wife, a husband is capable of "nourishing her"[133] with the grace he has received; for she is his body, and the grace which he has received he naturally gives to the rest of his body, that is, his wife and children.

This also is the special genius of a husband's headship, which Christ has established: Grace flows from God through the obedient head, which is the husband, to his body, which is his wife. A husband's male genius is not characterized by imposing rules and laws upon his wife, from which he himself is exempt, but rather in fulfilling God's law and being perfected by it. By means of experiencing the trial of temptation, you, my brother, will gradually become

---

[131]   Matthew 7:1-2
[132]   Hebrews 10:31
[133]   Ephesians 5:23

capable of mercifully encouraging you wife to do the same, and by means of such encouragement and assistance, you will transmit the grace of God to your wife.

# DAY 25

## The Divine Vision of Marriage

Recall, my brother, that the essential role of a husband is to establish the pace of self-giving love for his marriage, that the husband establishes this pace by imitating the pace of self-giving love established by Christ, and that if the wife follows this pace, it is most likely that the couple will achieve a united, harmonious, integrated front, to their own benefit and that of their children.

Marriage is the fountainhead and wellspring of the family. Strong marriages produce strong families. If you, my brother, desire to become a great father, you must first become a great husband. Many enemies of marriage will oppose you in this mission, but there are few as insidious as the tenacious, relentless, and consuming fire of lust.

Before discussing the evil of lust, a proper vision of marriage should be disclosed. It is not enough to know the enemies of marriage without understanding the elements which constitute a holy marriage. Often, well intentioned teachers err in describing the faith as what one should not do rather than what we are given the power to do.

By understanding the proper vision of marriage, the husband will more readily be inspired to become what he ought to be, namely, a husband in the image of Christ. Catching glimpse of this vision of authentic manhood, he will be more capable of fighting against what he should not be.

Before the institution of the Sacraments, before Christ established His Church, before the role of the prophets, before the calling of Israel, God intended to communicate and reveal basic knowledge of His divine identity to humanity.

From the beginning of creation God desired mankind to have knowledge of the inner mystery of the divine Godhead. Even by remaining mysterious to man, God inspired man to seek to know Him and His divine mysteries.

God, through Jesus Christ, "has revealed His innermost secret: God Himself is an eternal exchange of love, Father, Son and Holy Spirit, and He has destined us to share in that exchange."[134] God's plan, from the beginning of creation, was to share with humanity this mystery of the eternal exchange of self-giving love among the persons of the Trinity, so that mankind could comprehend its destiny of partaking in this eternal, self-giving, divine love.

God, by creating humanity to be comprised of both the male and female sexes, by granting the sexes a holy attraction toward one another for the sake of procreative union, instilled an inherent need within the human person to be drawn into self-giving communion, particularly expressed in the one-flesh union. The invisible, simple, incomprehensible God desired that mankind know the mystery of His three divine persons, so self-giving that they are eternally one essence; and so He proclaimed, "Let us make man in our image and likeness."[135] In other words, God created mankind as male and female, instilling within the human person a holy desire to give himself away to another in the authentic communion of marriage, so that, by experiencing the communion of persons in marriage, and particularly by begetting and raising offspring, each couple would become an image of the mystery of the divine communion of persons, which is the Trinity.

My brother, humanity cannot survive without male and female giving themselves away to one another in the one-flesh union. By

---

[134]   CCC 221
[135]   Genesis 1:26

creating us male and female, God created a symbol of the Divine Union, purposefully making it mandatory for a man and woman to become gifts to the other, to share and exchange themselves with one another in order to propagate the human race. By making us male and female, God allows humanity to discover that by entering into communion with one another in the covenant of marriage, human beings image God. Indeed, "man becomes the image of God not so much in the moment of solitude as in the moment of communion."[136]

My brother, God has created man with the inherent need to commune with another, particularly to become one flesh with his wife, and for this reason He has granted man an instinctive attraction toward the female sex. This desire for communion and this attraction toward woman, in its original character, and according to the original intention of God, is programmed by God into man to reveal the mystery of God to mankind.

The mere act of the one-flesh union, however, does not constitute the image of God, but rather the one-flesh union must be animated by the proper intentions on the part of the husband and wife if it is to become an effective image of God. Without the proper intention of the heart, that is, the choice to be a sincere gift to the other, the symbol of the one-flesh union is no longer a true sacrament, imparting efficacious power to sanctify the couple, but rather becomes an anti-sacrament, deforming the couple, maligning the goodness of their hearts, while also becoming an expressive antithesis of communion.

What then is the proper intention of the heart, and how should a husband love his wife sincerely? True Love is God, and God is true Love. The Trinity, for all married couples, is the ultimate model of self-giving love. God is three persons yet one God. Each of the divine persons is distinct, and yet all are completely united, one in

---

[136]   Pope John Paul II, *Theology of the Body,* 46

essence. Each divine person is His own person and yet is so self-giving that the three persons are completely one.

Love is One God, and God is three persons Who are One in Love. Each of the divine Persons is completely self-giving to the other, without being deprived of His distinct identity. Each divine Person has complete self-possession and therefore is able freely and entirely to give His Person to the other Persons of the Divine Godhead. Indeed, my brother, the Triune God teaches us that to give our person to another effectively we must possess our real person, for we cannot give what we do not have. The more a person possesses his real person, the more capable he is of giving that person to another and entering into an authentic communion of persons.

The Trinity is complete union and communion, a personal and eternal embrace of self-giving love, an unrestrictive integration of harmony. Our Lord bore witness to this divine communion when He said, "All that the Father has is mine."[137] And, speaking of the Holy Spirit, He said, "He will glorify me, for He will take what is mine and declare it you."[138] And, describing further His union with His Father, our Lord said, "Believe Me that I am in the Father and the Father is in me,"[139] and "I and the Father are one."[140]

God the Father, the Son, and the Holy Spirit, though distinct persons, are completely one in essence, and this triune God desires that man likewise be drawn into the divine communion of persons. Indeed, the union of the Trinity is fruitful, diffusive of love, bearing life to all creation. Our Lord confirms this fruitfulness by revealing the mission of God His Father: "I have come that you may have life more abundantly."[141] The Church echoes this benevolence of

---

[137] John 16:15
[138] John 16:14
[139] John 14:11
[140] John 10:31
[141] John 10:10

God, proclaiming the Holy Spirit as the "Lord and Giver of Life."[142] Considering this, we can conclude that the Trinitarian order of love, which human love should emulate, has the threefold character of being distinctive, unitive, and procreative.

In the beginning, man and woman constituted the primordial sacrament, the first sign of the Trinitarian order of love, by means of their personal distinction, their call to communion with the other, and their ability to be fruitful and multiply. If marriage and the marital act are to be an expression of God's self-giving love, they must maintain these three characteristics: distinction among persons, self-giving communion, and fruitfulness.

---

[142]   Profession of Faith

# DAY 26

## MAINTAINING DISTINCTION

To give yourself properly to your wife as an authentic gift, you, my brother, must have possession of your own person. Such possession of self is obtained gradually through the arduous process of self-mastery, which affords one the ability to give oneself to one's wife without objectifying her. By means of the Sacrament of Marriage, your person and your wife's person are bound as one. At the same time, each of you retains a personal identity distinct from that of the other. Without self-mastery, your distinctive personhood will inevitably become engulfed by your wife's person, or vice-versa. Indeed, if you reduce yourself to your instincts and passions, you will be overcome by lust for your wife, or for another woman, and rather than dominating your lusts, you will be dominated by them, reducing your dignity beneath that of an animal.

As we will see, my brother, a man's ability to maintain a distinct personality while achieving union with his wife is dependent upon his ability to maintain an elevation above his animal instincts. Therefore we will discuss two types of distinction, each dependent upon the other: first, that a man must remain distinct from his wife, while possessing himself through self-mastery in order to give himself away to her; and second, that a man must remain distinct from the animals in order to possess this power of remaining distinct from his wife. When a man submits to his disordered passions, he acts as though he is an animal, and losing his distinction from the animals, he also loses his distinction from woman, that male essence without which he is not capable of loving woman rightly.

In the beginning, Adam realized his distinction from the animal kingdom. Though "he might have reached the conclusion, on the basis of experience of his own body, that he was substantially similar to the other living beings," instead "he reached the conviction that he was 'alone.'"[143] Adam recognized that he was alone, that is, that he was different and distinct from the animals, by the fact that he was endowed with the capacity to love, and this love enabled him not to be bound by mere passionate instinct. Adam had the capacity to love, to be a sincere gift, to master his passions, and thus to ensure that he would uphold the dignity of a human companion's personhood.

You also, my brother, are above the animals, endowed with the capacity to love sincerely, given the ability to master your instincts and passions. You are not merely an animal, but rather a person created for union with God. The more you experience liberation from being dominated by your passions, the more you will possess your real person, and by possessing your real person, you will become capable of donating your person to your wife without being enslaved to using her for your own gratification.

By maintaining your distinction from the sphere of animals you will be able to remain distinct from the person of your wife while also being in full communion with her. By sincerely loving your wife from a position of self-mastery, you will keep your identity as a man intact, whereas if you lust after your wife (or any woman for that matter), your identity as a man becomes blurred by disordered passions. Whether you are being used by your wife, or using her, your manhood becomes distorted, cheapened, and animalistic. If you are master of self you will stand guard over your person, refusing to be mastered by concupiscence. By resisting the temptation to lust you will become a true man, a man who images the manhood of Christ.

---

[143] Pope John Paul II, *Theology of the Body*, 39

It is vital for men to understand that lust is the opposite of love. Lust uses the other for selfish reasons whereas love gives itself for the sake of the other. Lust reduces the desired person to a mere object, whereas love is the ability to deny one's disordered passions for the sake of the other. The man who has not undertaken the battle to defeat lust cannot accept and give love. The man who freely lusts is a slave to his passions and is incapable of experiencing the freedom to love.

It is also important that the two-fold aspect of lust be considered. Lust contains both an apparently negative and seemingly affirmative character, when in reality it is wholly disordered. Lust in its apparent goodness fills a man with the conviction that the woman's beauty exists solely to fulfill his sexual desires, while blinding him to the reality that this God-ordained attraction is meant to serve as a way for him to envision God's glory in the woman by seeing her entire person as it is transmitted through her physical beauty.

The reason that lust in this manner has an apparently affirmative character is that the man who is attracted to the beauty in his wife in this way can mask his disordered desire to possess her as an expression of marital love, or, at the very least, a compliment to her femininity.

Even the woman can be taken in by this deception, sensing the man's attraction and relishing such affirmation, though it bears the interior mark of lust. Though the male's desire to possess her is gravely disordered (for she is a person and not an object), it appears to her that he affirms her in desiring her.

Lust in its negative character assesses the woman by her physical attributes and finds her lacking the beauty, physical attributes, and sexual attraction that a man desires. In this case, the man commits the sin of lust by assessing the woman's body negatively, comparing her to an impossible standard of beauty, and finding her unsuitable for meeting his sexual desires and fantasies. By doing this, the woman remains, in the mind of the man, an object—though an unwanted object—because the man is unwilling to see and love her personhood, her entire being. This type of lust is negative in that the woman and her physical attributes are assessed and rejected by the man as a rejection of her entire person.

Lust, in either its apparently affirmative or negative sense, always attempts to separate or isolate the body from the person, convincing the mind of a man that the woman's body is an object created solely for his own pleasure; whereas love strives to see the person and God's image being expressed in and through her body.

Within the heart of nearly every man, the battle between love and lust rages; in fact, "in the heart is the battlefield between love and lust."[144]

As we will see, my brother, the real man decidedly enters the battle against lust with determination and faith, and by doing so wins the distinct glory of being a true man.

---

[144]   Pope John Paul II, *Theology of the Body*, 3

# DAY 27

## SELF-GIVING COMMUNION

"For this reason a man shall leave his father and mother and cleave to his wife and the two shall become one flesh; this is a great mystery, I mean in reference to Christ and His Church."[145]

A husband and wife, though they are two distinct persons, become one in marriage. This unity of a husband and wife is dependent upon the sincerity of their gift of self to one another. If a husband possesses himself and is master over his passions, he is able freely to give himself to his wife and experience more fully the spiritual and physical pleasure offered as a fruit of this intimate communion of persons.

Your goal, my brother, is to become able, by the power of the Holy Spirit, to give all that you possess to your wife, that the two of you may be fully one. In imitation of Christ, Who said to His Bride the Church, "all that the Father has is mine; therefore I said He will take what is mine and declare it to you," a husband gives all that he has received from God—including himself—to his bride, so that he and his wife become capable of forming a united front of love to their children.

If, however, the husband does not commit himself to undertaking the battle against lust, he will never possess himself, and not possessing his true self, he will attempt to possess his wife, which will lead to divisiveness and resentment within the marriage and inevitably within the entire family.

---

[145] Ephesians 5:23

By offering all that he possesses, which always first and foremost means himself, the husband becomes as Christ, capable of bringing Christ's healing, strength, power, confidence, and stability to his wife, who, by receiving these gifts, will more readily become an icon of the Church. If you, my brother, love your wife as though she is the Church, she will more readily become like the Church, "without spot or blemish."[146] Indeed, if you love like Christ you will become like Christ, "Who loved the church and gave himself up for her."[147]

Lust, as we will see, is the chief obstacle to a true communion of persons within marriage. If you become like Christ and your wife becomes like the Church, your family will be more capable of becoming a vibrant symbol of the self-giving, divine model of Trinitarian love.

---

[146]   See Ephesians 5

[147]   Ephesians 5:25

# DAY 28

## DISINTERESTED LOVE

If you, my brother, desire to be truly one with your wife and experience an authentic communion of persons in your conjugal union, you ought to strive with all of your intellect, will, and passions to love your wife in a disinterested manner.

By being disinterested, a husband strives with his entire being, both soul and body, to diminish all self-interest, redirecting all interest toward pleasing God by pleasing his wife. Indeed, the husband, by means of his actions and affections, must bear witness through his body that his only interest is his wife's true needs.

A husband's disordered self-interest, especially expressed within the marital act, will, over time, erode and numb the wife's sensitivity to her husbands' advances. If this occurs, even selfless acts of affection, offered by the husband, will more likely be misinterpreted by the wife as an appeal for self-gratification at her expense.

If a husband's self-interest intensifies, becoming a relentless desire for self-gratification, the husband and wife will begin to separate interiorly; and if this separation, in its early stage, is not checked, the distance between the two will become a measurable gulf, which will divorce the two in spirit. Eventually this spiritual distance will become a fissure into which the unsupported family will fall.

Indeed, your wife will inevitably view herself through your intentions. If your intentions are selfish, driven by lust, and impure, your wife will gradually view herself as an object to be used by her husband, rather than a person worthy of love. This absence of a husband's true, authentic, self-giving love will eventually erode her will to reciprocate love to her husband. Being viewed as an object, the wife is at risk of using herself as an object to obtain the affections of men.

Men are created with the innate desire to conquer, and often this desire to conquer is naturally, although erroneously, transferred to women and marriage. The husband, however, who "conquers" his wife by means of lust has already been conquered by his lusts. My brother, let there be no doubt, lust must be conquered or lust will conquer your marriage. Indeed, your wife is to be loved, not conquered, and to love, lust must be conquered.

Of what benefit is it if a husband has, by lust, satisfied his sexual "need," while his wife's heart is left unsatisfied? If a man is honest and has a conscience, he admits that even if he has obtained physical satisfaction by means of lust, he is spiritually dissatisfied that his wife is not satisfied in her heart, or that she has not experienced authentic love. He knows, in the depth of his being, that no real conquest has been accomplished. True satisfaction, for the husband, is knowing that he has done all in his power to satisfy his wife's need for authentic love. This is the conquest a man should desire: to conquer his disordered passions and ensure that his wife experiences love. Indeed, this is one of the most fundamental expressions of authentic manhood.

Many men mock the concept of self-conquest, because at the depth of their being they fear entering into the battle against selfishness. Indeed, this, for the man, is among the greatest of all battles, and is one of the greatest measures of true manhood.

True pleasure and satisfaction, experienced in the entire person—soul and body—during the one flesh union, can be accomplished gradually by means of disinterested marital love. Acts of love made with the hidden motive of self-gratification, however, although affording intimacy to a certain degree, also impede such intimacy, while affording a limited, momentary, hedonistic bout of physical pleasure, which, rather than bonding the entire persons of the two, encourages division. To the extent that the one-flesh union is mingled with lust, it will tend toward ill effects. The less lust intrudes upon this union, the more closely will the man be united to his wife.

My brother, your wife will respond more readily to your affections when she senses that she is of true value to you. Your gift of self to your wife is meaningful when she senses that you have repeatedly striven to overcome your disordered passions to love her rightly. The saying, "If you cannot say no, your yes means nothing," in this context is very appropriate.

By striving to conquer self-interest, and working with God's grace to love your wife in a disinterested manner, you will more readily experience the power, potency, pleasure, and holiness which God created the one flesh union to afford.

# DAY 29

FRUITFULNESS

"I have come that they may have life and may have it more abundantly."[148] This is our Lord's definitive statement, witnessing to the fact that God's love is not, and cannot be, void of life-giving power. Recall, my brother that created human love bears the divine image to the degree that it has the three marks of the Trinitarian order: distinction, unity, and fruitfulness. True unity between spouses is the fruit of authentic distinction, and true fruitfulness is the fruit of genuine spousal communion. Authentic communion between spouses is disinterested, seeking not its own needs, but rather striving to meet the needs of the other. When a husband and wife are determined to share the joys of self-giving, spousal love, they open themselves to the reward of spiritual and physical fruitfulness.

The natural fruit of conjugal love is life, and this life is experienced in the depth of the soul by means of the mutual affirmation of the other's person, as well as in the biological generation of new life. Openness and receptivity to the possibility of children as a consequence of conjugal love is inseparable from the life the spouses experience in their mutual affection, affirmation, and sincere love for the other. Just as the two persons become one in the conjugal act, so too, the life exchanged by the spouses and the life given in the person of a child constitute one life; the lives of the spouses unite in self-giving love to become incarnate in one flesh, the child.

---

[148]  John 10:10

This unity between the spouses and the fruit of their union raises the family to a symbol of the Trinity.

Though the couple's love reflects this Trinitarian order, often, due to natural causes, the couple may not experience the fruitfulness of a child. Despite the absence of the physical sign of this life, the spiritual life, as fruit of the communion of the spouses, still exists, though at times the lack of a child may be painful.

When, however, spouses use contraception to avoid the transmission of life, they not only deny the potential of bearing children, but also renounce the spiritual life afforded by the spousal communion of persons, because they have renounced the graced life of the Trinitarian order of love.

My brother, we must always remember that

> the body, in fact, and it alone, is capable of making visible what is invisible; the spiritual and divine. It was created to transfer into the visible reality of the world the mystery hidden since time immemorial in God, and thus to be a sign of it.[149]

The mystery hidden in God is the Trinity, the eternal exchange of divine persons, which God has chosen to reveal by means of the body in the union of the two becoming one flesh.

In this union of the husband and the wife

> it is the body itself which 'speaks'; it speaks by means of masculinity and femininity...it speaks...both in the language of fidelity, that is love, and also in the language of conjugal infidelity, that is of adultery.[150]

Therefore, spouses

> are called explicitly to bear witness – by using correctly the 'language of the body' – to spousal and procreative love, a witness worthy of

---

[149]   Pope John Paul II, *Theology of the Body*, 76

[150]   Pope John Paul II, *Theology of the Body*, 359

'true prophets.' In this consists the true significance and grandeur of conjugal consent in the sacrament of the Church."[151]

My brother, when expressing the depth of your love for one another by means of conjugal union, you and your wife communicate with your bodies your mutual consent to God and to one another; a consent to being receptive to life; an openness to the love of the Trinitarian God. This consent constitutes the truthful sign of God's love being imaged, transmitted, and communicated in your marriage.

However,

when the unitive and procreative meanings are willfully separated there is carried out….a real bodily union, but it does not correspond to the interior truth and dignity of communion of persons….Such a violation of the interior order of conjugal union, which is rooted in the very order of the person, constitutes the essential evil of the contraceptive act.[152]

From this, my brother, we can conclude that spouses "becoming one as husband and wife, find themselves in the situation in which the powers of good and evil fight and compete against each other." The "choices and the actions (of the spouses) take on all the weight of human existence in the union of the two."[153]

---

# DAY 30

## OVERCOMING TEMPTATIONS

If you, my brother, choose to become a great father by reconciling yourself to your vocation as husband and receiving your wife in her complete personhood, your resolve will inevitably be tested, particularly in your attempts to imitate the Trinitarian order. The areas in which you will be tested include those of achieving self-mastery and self-possession before giving yourself away, entering into communion with your wife in a disinterested manner, and always remaining open and receptive to the life which conjugal union may produce.

If you are determined to fulfill these three marks of the Trinitarian order, you will encounter the opposition of the incessant, relentless enemy known as lust. Lust, commonly experienced in the heart of every man, and apparently inherent to his condition and nature, is believed, by most men, to be a normal manner of living, an inseparable part of the male psyche, and even an acceptable way of relating to the female sex.

So common is man's acceptance of lust that many men believe it to be the power and evidence of their masculinity, thinking that without lust they cannot be a man.

Most men, however, recognize lust as socially and behaviorally unacceptable to the majority of the female sex, and therefore mask their lustful intentions with an exteriorly respectful demeanor, while internally maintaining the belief that lust is an integral part of manhood. Many men whose consciences have perceived the evils of lust in general erroneously believe it justifiable to use their wives for sexual gratification.

When a man marries a woman with this understanding, he soon discovers that his wife will limit her fulfillment of his disordered desires. Whether he realizes it or not, this is because she internally resists being used as an object. Even if initially the wife believes that she is being loved when her husband uses her to satisfy his sexual instinct, she eventually recognizes that such advances are not disinterested affections toward her but rather are only aimed at fulfilling his own interests.

When a wife perceives that her husband is not striving to love her in a disinterested manner, he will begin to suffer repeated rejections to his advances, disappointments to his pride, and sexual frustrations. If he does not check his disordered desires, he will eventually become resentful toward his wife.

Periods of prolonged abstinence due to a need to avoid pregnancy and the faithful renunciation of contraception, coupled with the already active male sexual faculty, will ultimately test a man and reveal his true intentionality. Just as one sees what lies under water as soon as its surface is calmed, so too when the joys of conjugal love cease, one can see clearly the intentionality of the husband's soul. Such prolonged periods of abstinence demonstrate to a man and his wife how deeply lust has rooted itself within his heart. This is especially true for a man who has already repeatedly engaged his sexual faculties. In the absence of the one flesh union, a man becomes keenly aware of his deep-seated self-interests.

Lust in the heart fuels self-interest, corrupting a man, debilitating his capacity to love selflessly. The husband who is bound by lust is prone to believe that he has license to obtain sexual satisfaction from his wife, that his lustful tendencies are normal, that these desires must be satisfied at all cost, and that he is not lusting after his wife, but rather demanding what is rightfully his.

Such a man believes that by "sacrificing" adultery in his heart with other women, he somehow has the right to use his wife to satisfy his sexual instinct. However, "adultery in the heart" is not committed only because the man looks in this way at a woman who is not his wife, but precisely because he looks in this way at a woman. Even if he were to look in this way at the woman who is his wife, he would commit the same adultery in the heart.[154]

A husband lusts after his wife, when he attempts to separate her person from her body, believing that her body alone is a good for him, rather than sacrificing his body for her greater good. Lust attempts to divorce love from sacrifice.

> Lust in the case of the husband toward his wife fundamentally changes the way in which woman exists "for" the man. It reduces the deep riches of her attractiveness as a female person to the mere satisfaction of the husband's need and thereby robs her of her dignity as a subject made in God's image. A man who uses woman's femininity to satisfy his own "instinct" has assumed the attitude "deep down," inwardly deciding to treat a woman in this way. This is precisely "adultery committed in the heart." So it is possible for a man to commit this adultery in the heart also with regard to his own wife if he treats her only as an object to satisfy instinct.[155]

In our pursuit of purity and the defeat of lust in our hearts, we once again turn to Abraham and Joseph, and by comparing the two, discover rich insights into how we may defeat this plague of lust and love woman rightly.

---

[154]   Pope John Paul II, *Male and Female He Created Them*, 298

[155]   Pope John Paul II, *Theology of the Body,* 157, 178.

# DAY 31

Recall, my brother, that a father's faith is demonstrated by a deliberate decision to reconcile with and dedicate himself to his wife, and then consequently to the offspring his wife bears. A husband whose marriage functions well, experiencing only minor challenges, may not sense an imperative to re-dedicate himself to his vocation as a husband. Trials, temptations, and sufferings, however, afford a husband the opportunity and challenge to commit himself more deliberately to his wife.

When a husband encounters a personal crisis, particularly within his marriage, his faith is tested and he is afforded an opportunity to discover or rediscover his true essence, which is to become a man who sacrifices himself on behalf of his wife and his God.

When a husband encounters a personal crisis, his faith undergoes a test of survival. My brother, without such a test no man can become a man of greatness. Truly, God uses a crisis to test a man with the purpose of inviting him to detach himself from his selfish tendencies and discover his essential masculinity. Within the storm of a crisis the husband is violently pressured to follow the temptation to preserve himself, even at times at the cost of his marriage and his fatherhood. Indeed, the evil one sows doubts in the mind of the husband, which if assented to, will lead him to seek liberation from his vocational responsibilities.

The evil one is determined to use a crisis situation to manipulate the husband and father into believing that he must abandon his vocational post to preserve himself, to find himself, while also whispering the alluring lie that he could do better, or that he does not deserve this. God, on the other hand, is continually promising and providing the necessary grace to overcome the insidious temptation, enabling the man to become a great father by being a great husband.

The evil one tempts the man to flee from his essential identity by denying his masculine essence, convincing him that real men should not be weighed down by such responsibilities, while also inciting him to cast off the yoke of marriage which unites him to his wife. A husband in this condition becomes especially vulnerable to violating his marriage by means of adultery and impurity of heart, believing that he has a right to be in love with another who apparently can give him happiness.

As stated previously, understanding your essence, yoking yourself to your wife, and striving for purity of heart are the three fundamental aspects of the husband's vocation. Indeed, if a husband understands his essence, he is more likely to remain yoked to his wife, and remaining yoked to his wife, he will be more determined to become pure of heart and love his bride as Christ loves the Church.

Purity of heart is directly associated with how closely a husband is yoked to his wife, and this bond cannot be properly forged unless the man understands his own essence.

Let us, my brother, return to the examples of Abraham and Joseph, and by typologically comparing the two, discover how they harkened to the call of their male essence, yoked themselves to their wives, engaged the battle for purity of heart, and by doing so, re-dedicated themselves to their vocation by receiving their wives and the offspring they bore.

# DAY 32

Abraham, our father in faith, expressed his faith by means of his obedience. Indeed, Abraham's obedience proved his faith, and his faith produced his obedience. As we have discovered, Abraham expressed his obedience to God by following the path marked out for him, though not knowing the way, and also by living as a stranger in the Promised Land. Yet it was amidst an intense personal crisis, concerning his wife and her condition of infertility, that Abraham's faith was tested and his obedience was proven, for "Sarai, Abram's wife, bore him no children."[156]

Abraham was eighty six years of age and Sarah, who was also advanced in age, had not borne him any children. Though the condition of Sarah's infertility was deeply distressing to the couple, even more perplexing was the meaning of the promise God had given Abraham, "Your own son shall be your heir."[157]

Abraham's vocational crisis stemmed from his desire to believe in God's promise to provide him an heir, combined with the reality of his wife's barren womb. Abraham experienced the personal tension between believing in what was seen, that is, Sarah's barrenness, and having faith in what was unseen, the divinely promised heir. Indeed, the elements which normally constitute a crisis appear to us as obstacles, when in fact they contain the concealed promises

---

[156]   Genesis 16:1
[157]   Genesis 15:5

of God, for whose saints "all things work together unto good."[158] Within the heart of Abraham, the visible obstacles and the unseen grace of God clashed in a battle for faith.

Precisely in this battle for faith Abraham was granted the opportunity to rediscover and grasp more deeply his essential role as a husband. Rather than leaving Sarah and obtaining a new wife, for decades Abraham denied himself and his desires and remained yoked to Sarah. Abraham continually re-affirmed his faith in God's promises while also remaining committed to his barren wife.

By suffering with Sarah and her condition of barrenness, Abraham bore her burden as his own, and rather than condemning her for her condition of infertility, he committed himself to her all the more. From Abraham we learn that to become a true husband, a true man of God, a man must suffer with his spouse, bearing her burdens as his own, even when such burdens apparently prove to be an obstacle to fulfilling profound and godly desires. Abraham, anchored in faith, believed in what was unseen in spite of what was seen, and, clinging to God, he clung to his wife. Indeed, by remaining steadfast in faith to God's promises Abraham was able to remain faithful to Sarah.

You, my brother, by clinging to God in faith, even when obstacles seem to be insurmountable, especially in regard to your wife and her burdens, will be given the grace to cling to her more faithfully and thus prove yourself a true man of sacrifice.

---

[158]    Romans 8:28

# DAY 33

Though Abraham remained faithful to God by remaining faithful to Sarah, always believing in the promises of God, the reality of Sarah's indefinite barrenness proved to be an obstacle which weakened her faith in God, tempting her to seek out a human solution to her problem of infertility. So Sarah, who "had an Egyptian maid whose name was Hagar, said to Abram, 'Behold now, the Lord has prevented me from bearing children; go in to my maid; it may be that I shall obtain children by her.'"[159]

Sarah's faith in the divine power and promise of God weakened, causing her to lose patience with God and His divine plan, which in turn caused her to resort to seeking an immediate solution to her personal dilemma. Indeed, Sarah compromised her faith in God by seeking a human solution to a divine problem, rather than believing that only a divine solution could remedy her human problem. Sarah surmised that God's fulfillment of the promised heir was delayed, and that therefore she must act with the power given her to provide an answer to their problem of infertility.

Sarah's crisis led her into a test of faith, which instead of strengthening her faith in God, proved to be an occasion for her faith to weaken, causing her to take matters into her own hands, seeking to control the situation. Sarah resolved to tempt her husband, who had learned to live from his masculine essence of

---

[159]   Genesis 16:1-2

self-sacrifice by remaining yoked to his wife, to have intercourse with her slave woman Hagar.

Sarah's directive was not a divine directive, but rather, human speculation, for she said, "it may be that I shall obtain children from her," indicating that this was human logic rather than divine wisdom.

> Abram hearkened to the voice of Sarai. So after Abram dwelt ten years in the land of Canaan, Sarai, Abram's wife, took Hagar the Egyptian, her maid, and gave her to Abram her husband as a wife. And he went in to Hagar and she conceived; and when she saw she had conceived she looked with contempt on her mistress. And Sarai said to Abram, "May the wrong done to me be on you! I gave my maid to your embrace, and when she saw that she had conceived she looked on me with contempt. May the Lord judge between you and me!" But Abram said to Sarai, "Behold, your maid is in your power; do to her as you please." Then Sarai dealt harshly with her and she fled from her.[160]

Notice, my brother, how the weakened faith of Sarah led Abraham to compromise his faith in God by accepting her human solution of taking Hagar, the slave woman, as his wife. The consequence of this worldly solution, which was not in union with the divine plan, was to multiply the dilemmas of Sarah and Abraham.

Indeed, though this act was understood as legal during the period in history in which Abraham had lived, based on a human custom which developed as a solution to infertility, Sarah and Abraham saw the fruit of putting their faith in human customs rather than the divine promise.

Often the laws of man, created as legal solutions to ease the difficulty of the burdens of life, contravene the divinely inspired law of God, which is always a law of love. The law of man can never replace God's law, upon which both it and we remain always dependent.

---

[160]   Genesis 16:2-7

For example, contemporary societies have embraced abortion as an ostensibly legal solution to the matter of unwanted pregnancies, and though this gravely immoral "solution" has appeared acceptable to many, it is in truth reprehensible when measured by the law of God.

The same holds true for human laws or customs condoning polygamy or infidelity, for Christ responded to the Pharisee's question about divorce by saying that "In the beginning it was not so," meaning that marriage has from the beginning of creation been comprised of one man and one woman. Christ also said "that every one who looks at a woman lustfully has already committed adultery with her in his heart."[161] These words of Christ, the definitive revelation of God, show that the custom of polygamy is contrary to God's will and the nature of marriage. Christ's standard is the only true standard of truth; anything less is bent at the destruction of marriage and fruitfulness. Even physical fruitfulness, if not in accordance with God's will, is barren of grace. This standard also applies to Abraham and Sarah and their crisis.

Though Sarah believed Abraham's intercourse with Hagar would be a remedy for her problem, the act instead increased her dilemma. In fact, Sarah had actually led Abraham away from the divine plan. The name Hagar means "to flee," and Sarah, having Abraham flee to Hagar, persuaded him to flee from God's will. By fleeing from God's will, Abraham and Sarah caused their marriage to become divided.

By handing her husband Abram over to her slave, Sarah submitted herself and her husband to the slavery of man's passions and lusts, and to the use of another human being as an object. Sarah's intention, the motivation of her heart, was to use Hagar, her slave woman, to obtain a child from her. Sarah was using Hagar as an object of production, attempting to extract a child from her, rather than loving

---

[161] See Matthew 5:28

Hagar for her own sake. By committing such objectification, Sarah was not only using Hagar, but also using her husband, silently asserting her right to use Abraham and Hagar to have a child.

We cannot, my brother, underestimate the rich symbolism contained in this account. Abraham, though strong in faith, allowed his prudential judgment to be weakened by Sarah's emotional reaction to their crisis, and thus he was moved from the freedom of faith to a disposition of slavery. Abraham allowed himself to be handed over to the slave woman, indicating that he reduced himself to using the slavish means of the flesh to achieve an apparent solution to his problem.

> For it is written that Abraham had two sons, one by a slave and one by a free woman. But the son of the slave was born according to the flesh, the son of the free woman (Sarah) through promise.[162]

By submitting to his wife's lust for children, Abraham submitted to lusting for the slave woman, thus submitting his own body to his slavish passions. As mentioned previously, although this act was considered a legal custom at the time, it proved to be an act that lacked divine grace; for rather than uniting Abraham and Sarah and binding their marriage, it caused dissension and division. Hagar, by conceiving, became contemptuous of Sarah, and Sarah, feeling Hagar's contempt, became contemptuous of Abraham. For his part, Abraham failed to protect the personhood and dignity of Hagar by releasing her into the power of a vengeful Sarah.

By submitting to the slavery of the flesh, that is, by submitting to our disordered passions in the vain attempt to resolve a problem, we become bound by the division such lusts cause. Lust spawns division, and division spawns lust. By recoiling from defending Hagar and her humanity and releasing her to Sarah, Abraham betrays the

---

[162]  Galatians 4:23

union of a man and wife, namely his union with his second wife Hagar, thus causing yet more division in the family.

My brother, how we respond to our sexual dilemmas truly sets the trajectory for the reception of our vocation. If a husband responds in faith, overcoming the emotional temptations to use illicit and erroneous solutions to resolve his dilemmas, he will be given the grace to be powerfully united to his wife. However, a husband will be tremendously disappointed with his marriage if he submits to the slavery of the flesh and allows the ways of lust to determine his solutions.

Such human solutions include using contraception to solve the problem of unwanted children, or in vitro fertilization to remedy the dilemma of wanted children, or divorce to solve the problem of sexual difficulties within marriage. All of these, though initially having the appearance of obtaining an immediate goal, have been statistically proven to cause division, divorce, familial breakdown, and behavioral chaos, all of which has led, family by broken family, to the degeneration of modern society. Lust spawns division and division spawns lusts. The man who stands at his vocational post, refusing to be dominated by lust, begins to reverse the tide of degeneration, and rather becomes a part of rebuilding the institution of marriage, the family, the micro-church, and eventually the Church as a whole.

Many men are duped into believing that man's ways are better than God's, for the solutions of men initially ease the pain caused by the problems of life. Abraham sought to ease Sarah's pain, yet by seeking an easier solution to the painful dilemma of infertility, he caused even more pain to Sarah, himself, Hagar, and later Ishmael, Hagar's son.

In the long run, the pain caused by taking matters into our own hands and resorting to illicit means to solve our quandaries is far greater than the sacrifice demanded by a Godly solution.

For example, a married man who struggles with lust and undergoes prolonged periods of abstinence experiences tremendous pain

in his attempt to die to his disordered passions and lustful dispositions. Initially, it may appear to be easier for him secretly to indulge
his lusts by use of pornography. However, such an illicit solution
leads to greater problems, such as lustful addictions, neglect of his
wife, and ongoing objectification of the human being. The pain
encountered in the long run is far greater and more damaging than
the initial sacrifice demanded.

The path of self-sacrifice and the purification of the heart from
the plague of lust may be painful, but the pain and damage caused
by an impure heart is far greater.

My brother, learn from the example of Abraham that God does
not make his covenant with, that is, He does not bind Himself in
approval of, man's illicit, erroneous, lustful solutions. In fact, God
rejects such contracts, agreements, and compromises, as he did with
Hagar's son Ishmael.

> And God said to Abraham, "As for Sarai your wife, you shall not
> call her name Sarai but Sarah shall be her name. I will bless her, and
> moreover I will give you a son by her; I will bless her and she shall
> be a mother of nations; kings of people shall come from her." Then
> Abraham fell on his face and laughed, and said to himself, "Shall a
> child be born to a man who is a hundred years old? Shall Sarah, who
> is ninety years old, bear a child?" And Abraham said to God, "O that
> Ishmael might live in thy sight!" God said, "No, but Sarah your wife
> shall bear you a son and you shall call his name Isaac. I will establish
> my covenant with him as an everlasting covenant for his descendants
> after him."[163]

Notice, my brother how Abraham still clung to the ways of man
rather than the ways of God by clinging to the human solution of
the slave child being approved as the promised heir. God, however,
steadied the wavering faith of Abraham, assuring him that Sarah,

---

[163]   Genesis 17: 15-19

his wife, would bear the promised son. In other words, man's ways and solutions are not necessarily God's ways, but it is necessary that God's ways become man's ways. How vital it is for the married man to live from this truth!

We must not submit to the slavery of this world by submitting to our lusts, but rather live in faith in the freedom of the promise of redemption, believing that God can heal our lustful hearts, making them capable of loving purely.

Indeed,

> we, brethren, like Isaac, are children of promise. But as at that time he who was born according to the flesh persecuted him who was according to the spirit, so it is now. But what does the scripture say? "Cast out the slave and her son; for the son of the slave shall not inherit with the son of the free woman." So, brethren, we are not children of the slave but of the free woman. For freedom Christ has set us free; stand fast therefore, and do not submit again to the yoke of slavery."[164]

If you, my brother, desire to become a great father, you must reconcile yourself to being fully committed to loving your wife in the way God intends. In other words, you must rely on the supernatural gift of faith, particularly in a crisis, believing that God's ways are not only achievable for us but are most beneficial and worthy of the sacrifice.

Within you, my brother, exist two sons, two men: one born of flesh, that is, of disordered passions, and the other born of spirit, that is, the inspiration of the Holy Spirit, which enables you to love purely. Only the husband who stands fast against the yoke of slavery to his passions, defeating the slavish man and his lustful disposition, will become a true man and thus raise his family to righteousness. Indeed, the man who has faith, believing that God will grant him

---

[164] Galatians 4:28-5:1

the necessary virtue of chastity, will experience the freedom for which Christ has set us free: the freedom to love rightly.

# DAY 34

Like Abraham's, Joseph's vocational crisis was linked directly to the order of procreation and the marital act. Abraham and Sarah had consummated their marriage, engaging in the one flesh union, yet bearing no fruit, whereas Mary and Joseph had not consummated their marriage, nor engaged in the one flesh union, and yet Mary was blessed with the "fruit of her womb," Jesus, the incarnate Word.

Whereas Abraham needed faith to believe that God would provide him and his wife a child, Joseph needed the gift of faith to believe that God had already provided the child in Mary. Both of these two patriarchal fathers' crises of faith existed in relationship to their wives and their wives' fruitfulness, or lack thereof; and salvation history depended upon whether or not these two men would endure the storm and tempest of their vocational crisis and discover their true essence and purpose as men by reconciling themselves to their vocation.

Faith cannot be proved without a crisis, and a crisis cannot be endured without faith. It was Joseph who, by enduring his vocational crisis, reconciled himself fully to Mary, his wife, and by "doing what the angel had commanded him,"[165] reconciled himself fully to God by embracing the child Jesus as his very own.

---

[165]   Matthew 1:24

Just as God promised Abraham, "Your wife shall bear you a son and you shall call him Isaac,"[166] so also God promised Joseph, "she (Mary) will bear a son, and you shall call Him Jesus,"[167] and trusting in this promise, Joseph "awoke and did what the Lord commanded him."[168]

My brother, it was precisely in this moment, while faced with great uncertainty regarding Mary's pregnancy, that Joseph lived from his essence, "doing" what was demanded of him, that is, deciding uncompromisingly to dedicate himself to, and sacrifice himself for, Mary and her Son, who would become also his son by means of this decision.

"'Doing' became the beginning of Joseph's Way."[169] Responding to God's call to fatherly greatness. Joseph did what he initially set out to do, that is, to love the Virgin Mary, not only by remaining betrothed to her, but also by sacrificing himself for her.

> Through his complete self-sacrifice, Joseph expressed his generous love for the Mother of God, and gave her a husband's 'gift of self.' Even though he decided to draw back so as not to interfere in the plan of God which was coming to pass in Mary, Joseph obeyed the explicit command of the angel and took Mary into his home, while respecting the fact that she belonged exclusively to God.[170]

Receiving the Virgin with child was Joseph's first step to receiving the Lord. In order to receive Jesus, Joseph first received Mary. Indeed, by receiving the Mother, he also received the Son, and by receiving one he received the other. Joseph's faith produced obedience and his obedience proved his faith.

---

[166]   Genesis 17:19
[167]   Matthew 1:21
[168]   Matthew 1:24
[169]   Pope John Paul II, *Redemptoris Custos*, 17
[170]   Pope John Paul II, *Redemptoris Custos*, 20

If you, my brother, also desire to become a man of God following Joseph's Way, the call to fatherly greatness, your faith must produce obedience, for "faith without works is dead."[171] Your first step of obedience is to receive your wife, yet not only your own wife, but also Mary, the wife of Joseph, "into your own home," that is into, the very temple of your soul. This first step is the key which unlocks holiness in your vocation. Indeed, if we bring Mary into our spiritual home, Satan will be crushed by her Seed, the seed that is Christ, Whom we also receive when receiving her.

By obeying God's command, Joseph submitted his life, his freedom, and his sexuality in all humility to God the Father, valiantly choosing to enter the battle to love Mary in a holy and disinterested manner, loving her as a daughter of God, as the spouse of God, and as the Mother of God. Joseph received and accepted his essential role to die to himself, his passion, and his conjugal rights in order to love Mary in a manner deserving of her profound dignity.

---

[171]  James 2:24

# DAY 35

### The Yoke of Mary and Joseph

Throughout the history of humankind, men have expressed either their undying strength and self-mastery, or their weakness and inability to master themselves, by means of their fidelity or infidelity to the woman given to them in marriage.

Indeed, the initial fall of humanity into error and sin by means of the serpent's alluring temptation was actuated by Adam's infidelity to Eve; that is, his unwillingness to defend, to cherish, to keep the garden of Eve. Rather, Adam, by means of his unwillingness to fulfill his manly essence, exposed his bride to Satan's insidious devices. By faulting at his post and failing to defend the sinless virgin, Eve, Adam denied his male essence as guardian of the garden, thus exposing not only Eve, but all of humanity, to the debilitating effects of shame, lust, and sin.

Consequently, the garden of Eve's interiority and dignity was invaded by the serpent, who infested this garden with death, lust, and sin. Bearing fruit from this garden, Eve bore the fruit of death to mankind and all creation.

In the fullness of time, at the end of the heritage of unfaithful men, God called a man from among men to be singled out as the forerunner of fidelity to the vocation of husbands and fathers, as the Guardian of the Garden of the sinless Virgin Mary. By answering this call, Joseph became the exemplar and human model of all married men and fathers.

This task to be the Guardian of the Virgin, to be the Guardian of the Garden, was presented to Joseph in an exceptionally painful, testing, and purifying manner. Indeed, how difficult it is for a common man to be the guardian of a wife who is faithful, unstintingly upholding her dignity without fail, whereas, for Joseph, his difficulties were multiplied by the fact that his betrothed was discovered pregnant without his participation.

Initially, the perplexed and tested Joseph withdrew, seeking an answer to the dilemma. Yet unlike the first Adam, he heroically retraced his steps in obedience, triumphantly defending his virgin Bride.

By deliberately making this decision to remain at his post, Joseph reconciled himself to his vocation as husband and father, overcoming the temptation to flee the garden of the Virgin. Joseph returned to the Garden to defend Mary from the serpent, the evils of men, their judgments and scrutiny. Standing beside her, Joseph became Mary's shield, her staunch defender, a pure and chaste husband who refused to "expose her to shame."[172]

Because of his protection of Mary, Joseph enabled the pure and spotless garden of life to bear the Fruit of Life, Jesus, for the salvation of all mankind. Indeed, this Fruit of her garden has brought life to all creation; for the fruit we eat is the "bread of life," that is, Christ's "flesh given for the life of the world."[173]

> In the words of the 'annunciation' by night, Joseph not only heard the divine truth concerning his wife's indescribable vocation. This 'just' man, in the spirit of the noblest traditions of the chosen people, loved the Virgin of Nazareth and was bound to her by a husband's love.[174]

In this act of love, Joseph yoked himself completely to Mary, uniting his heart and soul to hers.

---

[172] Matthew 1:20
[173] See John 6:51
[174] Pope John Paul II, *Redemptoris Custos*, 19 emphasis added

Analyzing the nature of marriage, both Saint Augustine and Saint Thomas always identify it with an 'indivisible union of souls,' 'union of hearts' with consent. These elements are found in an exemplary manner in the marriage of Mary and Joseph. At the culmination of the history of salvation, when God reveals his love for humanity through the gift of the Word, it is precisely the marriage of Mary and Joseph that brings to realization in full 'freedom' the 'spousal gift of self' in receiving and expressing such a love. In this great undertaking which is the renewal of all things in Christ, marriage too is purified and renewed – becomes a new reality, a sacrament of the New Covenant. We see that at the beginning of the New Testament, as at the beginning of the Old, there is a married couple. But whereas Adam and Eve were the source of evil which was unleashed on the world, Joseph and Mary are the summit from which holiness spreads over all the earth. The Savior began the work of salvation by his virginal and holy union, wherein is manifested his all–powerful will to purify and sanctify the family-that sanctuary of love and cradle of life.[175]

My brother, look to Joseph, who fully yoked his heart and soul to Mary, to learn how you ought to embrace your vocation as husband and father by yoking yourself fully to your bride. By means of Joseph's marriage to the Virgin and his fathering of Christ, marriage and family have been renewed as a means of sanctification and holiness, making you also, by God's grace, a minister of God's grace to your family.

---

[175]   Pope John Paul II, *Redemptoris Custos*, 7 emphasis added

# DAY 36

In her litany of praise, the Church proclaims St. Joseph the "Chaste guardian of the Virgin," "Joseph most Chaste" and the "Guardian of Virgins." The vocation of husbands and fathers was purified and renewed by God in the person of St. Joseph, who stands as a redeemed type of the old Adam, and thus deserves the title "Guardian of the Garden."

It was Joseph's glory and duty and obligation to enter spiritually the holy garden of Mary, by means of their union of wills and hearts, without entering her garden bodily. By entering the Garden of the Virgin in this manner, Joseph also entered the battlefield of lust, exercising, by the power of the Holy Spirit, self-mastery in thought and action. In the words of Pope John Paul II,

> Are we not to suppose that *(Joseph's) love as a man was also given new birth by the Holy Spirit*? Are we not to think that the love of God which has been poured forth into the human heart through the Holy Spirit molds every human love into perfection? By this love God also molds – in a completely unique way – the love of husband and wife, deepening within it everything that bespeaks an exclusive gift of self, a covenant between persons, and an authentic communion according to the model of the Blessed Trinity.[176]

Indeed, the union of Mary and Joseph with the child Jesus, which we are called to imitate and which we can participate,

---

[176]  Pope John Paul II, *Redemptoris Custos,* 19 emphasis added

constitutes the deepest human expression of Trinitarian love. Recalling the three marks of Trinitarian love—distinction, unity, and fruitfulness—we discover the faithful example of Joseph, who so decisively differentiated himself from the animal realm and exercised self-mastery by overcoming his disordered passions, enabling him to achieve self-possession, which in turn enabled him to give himself away fully as a complete gift of self to Mary, thus giving their marriage the power to bear the most abundant life conceivable. This example of Trinitarian love within the Holy Family could not have been given without Joseph's deliberate intention to sacrifice himself, his passions, and his lusts in order to love Mary properly.

My brother, as mentioned previously, often a man seeks man-made solutions to resolve his battle for purity rather than abiding in the Trinitarian order of love. Many men seek the path of least resistance, and never attain the glory of victory in the battle to love with sincerity and disinterestedness. The path of least resistance is the road to non-glory, mediocrity, and a banal life. The love demanded to love like the Trinity is at first painfully sacrificial, but if sought with perseverance, it will afford joy, glory, vitality, and peace.

The path of least resistance is the road to hell, a road leading into nothingness, whereas the road of the Trinitarian order is the road of the Holy Spirit, a road of purification, of training, and of victory. Just as our Lord was "led by the Spirit about the desert for forty days, being tempted the while by the devil,"[177] so too we must be led by the Holy Spirit into periods of training and purification if we are to fulfill our vocation as husbands and fathers.

God calls you, my brother, to follow the Spirit to the promised land of fatherhood by means of the route of the purifying wilderness of the husband's vocation. If a man embraces his vocation as husband, he will become more capable of embracing his vocation

---

[177]   Luke 4:1

as father, but the power to fulfill such a tremendous vocation can only be obtained by means of the Holy Spirit. Therefore, let us, my brother, follow the faithful, chaste example of Joseph, who, led by the Holy Spirit, was faithfully obedient to the ways of God, and was granted the grace of internal transformation, that is, the ability to love the Virgin in a redeemed manner, without being bound by lust.

"Joseph Most Chaste" set the pace for his marriage and, even today, continues, from heaven, to set the pace for all husbands in their efforts to love their wives in a redeemed manner. "Joseph Most Faithful" sets the standard for all husbands in their faith, demonstrating that our generous God, by the power of His Holy Spirit, desires to redeem our sexuality and have such redeemed sexuality bear fruit.

This too, my brother, is our call, our rule: To receive the Holy Spirit, with Mary, as Joseph did, and by doing as he did, to become what he became: a man who overcame and defeated lust, loving his bride and defending the garden. When we receive such grace, our family will be able to become holy as the Holy Family became. Indeed, "the Church deeply venerates this Family, and proposes it as the model of all families."[178]

---

[178]   Pope John Paul II, *Redemptoris Custos*, 21

# DAY 37

BECOMING A GUARDIAN OF THE GARDEN

As you can see, my brother, to become a Guardian of the Garden is among the most demanding and yet graciously rewarding callings that God can offer a man, for this calling requires that the husband be responsible for protecting his wife's sacred dignity, just as Christ protects and animates His bride, the Church. By defending sacred womanhood, particularly his own wife's sacred dignity, a man defends not only his own wife, but also, by default, his entire family.

A father's purity and love is like a burning coal, which heats the furnace of love within the family, and from this furnace, saints are formed, who by God's grace assist in the transformation of the world.

Without authentic and virtuous human fatherhood, it is gravely difficult for a child to even begin to understand the true identity of God as Father.

For this reason we must become like Joseph, sincere men who, by invoking God's mercy, become capable, by the power of the Holy Spirit, of defeating lust. Only by the power of the Holy Spirit are the defeat of lust and the attainment of purity possible. With the Holy Spirit, however, a husband is capable of becoming a redeemed man who repeatedly defeats lust, and by doing so, he unlocks the glory which lays hidden in the person of his wife. As a husband loves his wife purely, her dignity is re-discovered, restored, and even exalted, thus granting her the security and confidence to un-guard herself and thus reveal the true, beautiful, and glorious woman God created her to be.

In the game of American football, a receiver runs a pattern, setting his course in stride, without turning back, trusting that when he finishes his pattern and turns his glance toward the quarterback, the quarterback will have thrown the ball accurately into his hands; and if the receiver is ready, he will catch the pass and continue on toward the goal. In the life of faith, we are asked by God to run many patterns with no ball in our arms. We appear somewhat foolish to by-stander as we fly with great speed in route toward the destination to which God has called us—without any ball in hand. We are running toward the goal line, and yet we do so without the ball that makes reaching the goal of value. Yet we must trust in God, Who is a faithful quarterback, believing that He not only has set us on our pattern, but will also provide the perfect pass, squarely landing grace in our spiritual hands, ensuring that we may cross the goal line with the provided grace in hand.

A man must run the pattern of purity, and he must set his course without turning back, trusting, though empty handed at times, that God will provide, by the power of His Holy Spirit, the necessary grace to defeat lust, attain purity, love his wife sincerely, and raise his children to holiness, thus crossing the goal line and attaining victory. Only by faith will a man defeat lust – only by the Power of the Holy Spirit will a man become pure. The Prayer of Faith is the means by which we must run our pattern, that is, pursue our vocation of fatherhood, believing that the Holy Spirit will answer this prayer with unspeakably profound redemptive grace.

As stated previously, the marriage of Mary and Joseph, with Christ as the fruit of this love, constitutes the closest human image of the Triune God's love. Therefore if you, my brother, desire your family to become a symbol of the Trinity, you must first take Mary, the Spouse of the Holy Spirit, into your heart, receiving her as your own Mother. In doing so, you will also receive the Child she has received, and in this you will also be following the humble yet heroic example of Joseph. Thus you will begin to establish your family as a beacon of the Light of God's Triune Love.

Though Joseph was completely continent, he nevertheless serves as the primary example of purity and chastity for all married men; for if the chaste life of Joseph can be the "first witness of a fruitfulness altogether different than the flesh, that is, of a fruitfulness of the Spirit: 'That which is conceived in her is of the Holy Spirit,'"[179] then we too, when we beget physical life by means of chaste and pure love, can also beget spiritual life in our marriage and family.

Joseph's chaste example teaches the husband that by loving his wife in a disinterested manner, he will be free to love her rightly, and in doing so, the husband will allow his marriage to bear spiritual life.

> The marriage of Mary and Joseph conceals within itself, at the same time, the mystery of the perfect communion of persons, of the man and woman in the conjugal pact, and also the mystery of that singular continence for the kingdom of heaven: a continence that served, in the history of salvation, the most perfect 'fruitfulness of the Holy Spirit.' It was, in a certain sense, the absolute fullness of that spiritual fruitfulness, since precisely in the ...pact of Mary and Joseph in marriage and in continence, there was realized the gift of the Incarnation of the Eternal Word.[180]

By being chaste, my brother, you will become capable of achieving a true communion of persons with your wife, and this communion cannot help but to transmit the fruitfulness of the Holy Spirit, "the Lord and Giver of Life." If you desire love, joy, and peace to reign in your marriage and family, then decide today to love your wife with the purity of St. Joseph.

[179]   John Paul II, *Theology of the Body*, 268
[180]   ibid

All husbands are not called by God, like Joseph, to complete continence, yet all husbands are called to be chaste. During periods of continence and abstinence, however, the virtue of chastity is gravely tested. These periods of abstinence, wherein no physical union occurs, may initially appear to be difficult to endure, but by the grace of God, they can become sweet and fruitful, enabling the husband to experience his true masculine dignity, while also bearing spiritual life for his marriage and family.

My brother, especially during such times of testing, "offer your body as a holy and living sacrifice to God"[181] upon the altar of your marital bed, denouncing Satan and his temptation to objectify your wife, or any other woman for that matter. The God Who is "near to all who call upon Him, to all who call upon Him in truth,"[182] will provide you the grace and power necessary to become a redeemed man who, like Joseph, refrains from exposing his wife and her garden to the shame of lust.

In this matter of purity, your fatherhood depends upon your doing what the Lord commands you. Indeed, Joseph's love for Mary and his doing what the Lord commanded him enabled Joseph to not only be the model for all husbands, but also the exemplar father for all fathers. Indeed,

> in this family (the Holy Family) Joseph is the father: his fatherhood is not one that derives from begetting offspring; but neither is it an 'apparent' or merely 'substitute' fatherhood. Rather, it is one that fully shares in authentic human fatherhood.[183]

Your fatherhood, my brother, is not defined by physically begetting children, but rather by how you share the faith you have received with the children God gives you. The faith that you share

---

[181]   Romans 12:1

[182]   Psalm 145:18

[183]   Pope John Paul II, *Redemptoris Custos*

is a faith in the God Who "is able to do all things more abundantly than we desire or understand, according to the power that worketh in us,"[184] including the power to make us pure of heart.

---

*Sacrifice*

# DAY 38

A Father's Ultimate Expression of Obedience

Brother in Christ, God gives rewards for our faithfulness, expecting us to reward others by sacrificing the reward He has given us. By receiving a blessing from God, we are promising to bless others with the blessing received. When a man receives a child from God, he must acknowledge that the child is not his own but is a child of God. While it is true that the child of the earthly father is from his father's flesh and blood, the father is never to claim ownership of the child. No person can be reduced to a possession of another. Children can never be possessed by parents as objects, for they are created and willed by God for their own sake. We are all children bearing children, for "There is only one Father in heaven," and we are children in relation to Him. God the Father has entrusted his very own children to children who are fathers, relying upon them to nourish, strengthen, admonish, and prepare them to become true sons of God in the Son of God.

The ultimate act of obedience, for a father, is to sacrifice his own child as the eternal Father sacrificed His only begotten Son for each of us. This sacrifice, of course, is not to be confused with offerings akin to the killing of the first-born, which the Canaanites and other pagan cultures offered to their false gods. Far from taking life away from his own child, a father is called to give his child life, thus enabling his child to become "a holy and living sacrifice unto the Lord."[185] Look around you, brother, and see how fathers have

---

[185] Romans 12:1

chosen to sacrifice their children as the pagans have done, foolishly believing that they are giving their children life. Many fathers neglect to protect their children from evil influences, permit them to avoid developing a strong work ethic, and indulge them with an over-abundance of material gifts. By doing such things, fathers believe that they are "letting the child live," but instead they are sacrificing their children to the vices of fallen men. How often have you heard a person say to a father who is striving to defend his children from morally harmful influences, "Just let them live, let them be children." Brother, those who allow their children ready access to morally harmful influences, though they believe that they are "letting their children live" and "letting them be children," are in reality allowing the child's soul to die, losing the purity of childhood. A father grants life to his child by instilling in the child virtue rather than vice.

A father who teaches his child the value of sacrificial love enables his child to be given in sacrifice to God. Far from extinguishing the life of the child, this pedagogy of sacrifice gives the child something for which to live. "Christ fully reveals man to himself and makes his supreme calling clear."[186] In Christ, each man sees the sacrifice that he is called to emulate, and looking to that example of sacrifice he discovers meaning for his own life. When a father, by example, teaches his child the art of sacrificial love for the benefit of others, the child does not lose life but gains the life that he can freely give. "Man only finds himself by becoming a sincere gift,"[187] but the more one is selfish, the more lifeless he becomes. The giving of oneself selflessly gives life to the one who gives, while the one who selfishly keeps life to himself extinguishes the little life he has. Though a man has light, if he hides it, keeping it only for himself, it cannot be seen, not even by the one who hides the

---

[186]   *Gaudium et Spes*, 22

[187]   *Gaudium et Spes*, 24

light. In hiding the light he either extinguishes it—for it needs air to keep aflame—or, holding it too closely, burns himself; but if he chooses to expose the light, sharing it with others, how bright does the light become!

My brother, a man who has learned the art of sacrifice has learned the art of love, and the man who loves is fully alive. It is the role and mission of each father to teach his child how to become fully alive by teaching his child how to die to himself. By studying Joseph, through the type of Abraham, we will enter into the very heart of fatherly sacrificial love, gaining for ourselves a fresh direction and inspiration for our vocation as fathers.

# DAY 39

## The Three Stages of Sacrificial Discipleship

Building upon the premise that the prayer of faith is comprised of silence and obedience expressed in sacrifice, we will now explore the three stages of fatherly sacrifice: the initiating, unitive, and vicarious stages. We will examine the first two stages, in which a father introduces his child to suffering and trains his child in the art of self-sacrifice, first through the fatherly model of Abraham, and second through the example of St. Joseph. After this, we will proceed to study the third stage, by meditating upon both Abraham's and Joseph's vicarious sacrifice through their sons as a type of the vicarious sacrifice of the Heavenly Father through His only begotten Son.

My brother, this preparatory study of these three stages will enable us to see more clearly how Joseph the faithful father is the fulfillment of Abraham our father in faith, and how Joseph's fatherhood is a fulfillment of the prefiguring father Abraham, while also being a type of the Heavenly Father Who ultimately fulfilled these stages of fatherly sacrifice, which neither Joseph nor Abraham could completely fulfill. This study will provide useful and inspiring knowledge, aiding our own pursuit of the task of preparing our children to be other Christs, while also enabling us to embrace the comforting truth that God the Father Himself has already met the sacrificial demands of the law, thus endowing our own fatherhood with the grace to fulfill the law of love.

# DAY 40

## ABRAHAM'S SACRIFICE:
### A TYPE OF JOSEPH, A TYPE OF THE HEAVENLY FATHER

"The Lord visited Sarah as he had said, and the Lord did to Sarah as he had promised. And Sarah conceived, and bore Abraham a son in his old age at the time of which God had spoken to him."[188] Abraham's persevering penetration into the darkness of the unknown future seemed to have ended with the dawn of Isaac's life. Faith in the unseen promise of the Lord to provide an heir had been rewarded and made visible in the child Isaac. The darkness and questioning that loomed within the mind and heart of Abraham diminished as Abraham and Sarah rejoiced in their child, whose name meant laughter. For a season, Abraham rejoiced in the life of his son, nourishing, teaching, and guiding the child to manhood. The patriarch of great faith lived much of his life in a desert of spiritual dryness, "hoping against all hope"[189] that his prayers for an heir would be answered. Soon after this period of intense spiritual darkness, the veil was lifted, allowing Abraham to rejoice in the spiritual consolation that God had given him. His consolation was crushed, however, by the command from God: "Take your son, your only son Isaac, whom you love, and go to the land of Moriah, and offer him there."[190]

Friend, if we put aside any pseudo-Christian idealistic nostalgia and consider Abraham's plight squarely, we will discover the

---

[188]  Genesis 21:1-2
[189]  Romans 4:18
[190]  Genesis 22:2

truth about what is necessary to become a great father. For decades Abraham held fast to the Lord's promise, believing that God would grant him an heir in whom his descendants would be as numerous as the stars. Indeed, God fulfilled the long awaited promise, but no sooner had Abraham rejoiced in the fulfillment of the promise than the promised one was commanded by God to be sacrificed.

Familiarity with the account of Abraham's offering of Isaac may tempt us to remain upon the surface of the story without entering into it more deeply, but this does us a grave injustice if we are desirous of obtaining knowledge of the heart of fatherhood. We cannot underestimate the turmoil that overcame Abraham's being. Though the scripture states simply that "Abraham rose early in the morning... and went to the place where God had told him,"[191] we must be careful not to believe that Abraham was insensitive to what was commanded of him. Scripture often relates events or occurrences in brief statements that, if misinterpreted, can lead us to believe that the event was unimportant or lacking in human emotions and sentiment. References such as "Pilate had Him scourged"[192] demonstrate to us that, though the words are few, the reason is because the sentiments are too great to disclose. There is no doubt that Christ's scourging was beyond all telling, as were Abraham's sentiments at having to sacrifice "his only son, whom he loved."[193]

What thoughts raced through the mind and heart of father Abraham between the time of the command and the climbing of mount Moriah? Did Abraham simply believe that God was like the gods of the pagans, who demanded human sacrifice as fitting worship? Did Abraham believe that, after killing Isaac, God would raise his dead son back to life? As the author of the letter to the

---

[191]   Genesis 22:3

[192]   John 19:1

[193]   Genesis 22:2

Hebrews tells us, "He considered that God was able to raise men even from the dead; hence he did receive him back and this was a symbol."[194] We do not know the precise thoughts, temptations, and doubts that barraged Abraham's mind in the face of this command; but we are assured of his faith, expressed unhesitatingly in complete submissiveness.

Abraham's rising early the next morning to carry out the command issued from God indicates his eagerness to complete what was demanded of him. This eagerness hints that, despite his love for his son, Abraham had keen knowledge of his own sinfulness. Brother, the example of our father in faith teaches us that only a true knowledge of self and one's sinfulness before God allows one to assume the proper posture of humble submission, not questioning God or grumbling against His command. The sacrifice of Abraham became acceptable, not because it was his son Isaac whom he was offering, but because his "sacrifice was a humble contrite heart, which the Lord did not spurn."[195]

There are those who believe that Abraham did not persevere in faith as far as he should have. They suggest that Abraham would have demonstrated more faith by calling the faithful God to faithfulness to life by requesting the preservation of the life of Isaac immediately. They assume that if the patriarch had stood in the breech between God and Isaac, Isaac's and Abraham's relationship would have been shielded from damage. Because of Abraham's fear of questioning God, they contend, he did not demonstrate as much faith as he ought to have had, and consequently caused Isaac's faith in his father to be lost, inflicting great distress to the young man.

Dear brother in Christ, a closer study of Scripture will show that this is foolishness. What effect did Abraham's silent submission have on his son Isaac? After examining the lives of the

---

[194] Hebrews 11:19

[195] See Psalm 51:17

Patriarchs, we discover that only the patriarch Isaac was spared from being sent into exile. Exile was the punishment given to one who demonstrated unfaithfulness to God's covenant, and often this covenant was violated in regards to fidelity to a God-given spouse. Isaac was the only Patriarch who was not sent into exile, and also the only patriarch who was completely faithful to his God-given bride. Far from Abraham's faithfulness driving Isaac away from God, Abraham's faith instilled faith in Isaac. Isaac witnessed, first-hand, that to those who are faithful to God, God is faithful in return, "for He cannot deny Himself."[196] The act of his father's faithfulness was forever imprinted upon the soul of Isaac, continually prompting him to faithfulness before God.

Often, fathers are convinced that by disciplining their children in obedience to God they will damage the child, causing the child to become disobedient. From Isaac, however, we learn that the child who witnesses unwavering faith in his father will live by faith, for faith is an act of discipline that begets love, and discipline is an act of love that begets faith. "For the Lord disciplines him Whom He loves, and chastises every son whom He receives."[197] Because of Abraham's example, Isaac understood that submission to the Creator always takes precedence over any love for the creature.

Do not become like those fathers who neglect disciplining and instructing their child in ways of holiness in favor of maintaining friendship with the child. Those who neglect their children by neglecting to discipline them will receive discipline from the Father, as a natural consequence, when they are neglected by their own children who refuses them holy submission. In their attempts to maintain friendship at the cost of instruction, such fathers lose true friendship with their own children as well as the friendship and instruction that comes from God. Be faithful, brother, in raising

---

[196] 2 Timothy 2:13 "If we are faithless He remains faithful,"
[197] Hebrews 12:6

your children to faith, and in consequence your children will most likely not only be faithful to you, but most importantly, faithful to God. By means of discipline and instruction in the virtuous life, the faithful father sacrifices apparent friendship with his child in exchange for the hope of affording his child friendship with God. This sacrifice of a father enables his child to become sacrificial, offering himself as a "holy and pleasing sacrifice unto the Lord"[198] for the sake of his own earthly father, and, most importantly, for the Heavenly Father's sake.

---

[198]   Romans 12:1

# DAY 41

"And Abraham took the wood of burnt offering, and laid it on Isaac his son;" and Isaac said to his father Abraham, "My father!"[199]

My brother, notice that it was Abraham, the father, who laid the wood for the burnt offering, often seen by the Church Fathers as a type of the cross, upon the body of Isaac, his son. This wood is not only a symbol of the cross of Christ, which the Heavenly Father laid upon His Son Jesus, but is also a symbol of the cross of discipline that every father is to place squarely upon the spiritual shoulders of his own child. Abraham's act of placing the wood upon the body of Isaac proclaims that every father has been ordained, by means of his vocation, to initiate the first signs of sacrificial love in his own child. Dear brother, how difficult this is for fathers who have tender hearts, or worse, for a father who foolishly desires to choose friendship with his child over choosing the will of God! My brother, do not let fear of losing your child's love be the cause of succumbing to the temptation of avoiding the task of laying the wood of discipline upon your child. Do not fear the demands of preparing your child for sacrifice, believing that the child's love for you will be lost. A father who prepares his child to lose his life by means of sacrificial love will not lose the child's love, but by choosing to sacrifice the false love of apparent friendship, will enable his child to gain life, thus winning the love of his child in the end.

---

[199] See Genesis 22:7

Brother, it is vital that we embrace the fact that this type of initiation will often cause the child pain, and in causing the child pain will also cause the father's heart distress. But this must not deter us from providing this initiation in a consistent and dedicated manner. If we choose to bury this truth, we are not viewing the filial relationship between father and child through the lens of reality, but are deceiving ourselves, seeing the relationship for what it is not rather than what it truly is. Listen, my brother, to the words of Isaac, who, despite the burden of the wood of discipline, was moved to call out, "My father!"[200] Isaac's affectionate salutation, "my father!", is a proclamation that a child who receives the cross of discipline from his father will indeed claim his father as his own. Isaac did not reject his father or spurn the burden of the wood, but graciously responded to his father with filial respect, because his father granted him the responsibility to participate in worship by carrying the wood of sacrifice. A father who disciplines his son claims him as his own, and a son who is disciplined claims his father as his own, "for what son is there whom his father does not discipline? If you are left without discipline, in which all have participated, then you are illegitimate children and not sons."[201] Introducing the child to faith by initiating suffering through discipline, a father legitimizes his fatherhood as an authentic resemblance of the Eternal Father's fatherhood and legitimizes his child's sonship as an authentic symbol of Christ's eternal Sonship.

---

[200]   ibid
[201]   Hebrews 12 :7-8

# DAY 42

### ABRAHAM'S AND ISAAC'S UNITIVE SACRIFICE

"And he said, 'Here am I, my son.'. . . So they went both of them together."[202]

Dear brother, it would be scandalous for a father who has introduced his child to the art of sacrificial love to promptly remove his aid, leaving the child to embrace sacrifice on his own accord. Rather than teaching the child the art of sacrificial love, this removal of assistance would convey a denial of the embrace of the cross, for the cross of a loved one is indeed the cross of the those who love the loved one, and a cross of a son is not the son's only but the father's cross as well. Training of one's child in the art of sacrifice does not end with an introduction to discipline, but continues through a commitment to walk alongside the child, encouraging the child to pursue the only reasonable goal: to become one with his father in Christ's sacrifice.

After Isaac called out to his father, Abraham responded, "Here am I my son,"[203] indicating Abraham's unshakable fidelity to his son. By remaining close to his son, Abraham was assuring his son of his love for him, but also ensuring that his son fulfilled the task of carrying the wood of sacrifice while simultaneously carrying the sacrifice of himself to be given upon the wood. Like Abraham, every father is called to walk the hill of Moriah or Calvary with his child, helping the child to fulfill the task of self-sacrifice.

---

[202]  Genesis 22: 7-8
[203]  Genesis 22:7

It is reasonable to believe that Abraham was tempted to free himself from his son's side, or tempted to free his son from his side, thus freeing his son from being the sacrificial offering. Abraham, however, did not allow this temptation of false freedom to hinder his fidelity to God and the command to sacrifice his only son whom he loved. Choosing not to free his son from the burden, Abraham freed himself and his son from the burden of disobedience. Burdened with the wood of sacrifice, Isaac was no longer burdened with the fear of being the sacrifice, for he embraced his fear by freely becoming the sacrifice. Though this unitive obedience offers great freedom from the burden of disobedience, it also entails a sadness of heart that is caused by the looming separation which is a direct result of the sacrifice. Despite this, a father must not fear setting the heavy burden of the cross upon his child, but only fear not helping to carry the burden once it has been placed upon the child. Abraham's fidelity to Isaac declares the duty that each father has to prepare his child for sacrifice, to travel the road to Calvary with him, and to help his child achieve the goal of becoming a "holy and living sacrifice unto the Lord."[204]

---

[204]   Romans 12:1

# DAY 43

"At the end of eight days when He was circumcised, He was called Jesus,"[205]—"And he (Joseph) called His name Jesus."[206]

While it is true, my dear brother, that the scriptures do not mention specifically whether or not Joseph himself circumcised Jesus, the scriptures do indicate that Joseph named the child at the time of the child's circumcision. From this we can infer that Joseph either presented the child to the person who circumcised Jesus or performed the circumcision himself. For many reasons, this fact is of great importance.

First, Joseph brought the Son of the God Who established the old Covenant with man into the old Covenant, effecting man's fulfillment of the old Covenant in Christ. The Word of God united Himself with flesh, integrating the divine and human natures into one Person. This Person, by means of this union, fulfilled all demands of the old law in His own flesh. It has been said that the salvation of man could have been purchased with a single drop of Christ's blood, leading us to believe that man's salvation could have been purchased during Christ's circumcision, when Christ's blood was first spilled. What man could not do for himself, Jesus, as man, did for man; for man could not fulfill the law of God, but God, as man, fulfilled the law perfectly. And yet Jesus, as a babe, was not capable of fulfilling the Old Law independently of man, for he was

---

[205] Luke 2:21
[206] Matthew 1:25

dependent upon a man to grant Him entrance into the Covenant. Christ chose not to save man independently of man, but became a man dependent upon man, and with man, saved man. Jesus needed a man to help Him fulfill the law of God, and this man was Joseph. No man except Christ could have saved mankind from the consequences of sin, yet Christ, in His humanity, saved man from sin by the help of His earthly father Joseph.

Although Christ in His divine nature is absolutely independent of man, He freely willed to become dependent upon man by becoming man, for "Christ became like us in all things except sin."[207] Becoming like us in all things, he became dependent upon man like every man. This, my brother, includes Christ's utter dependence upon his father, Joseph, to initiate His own sacrifice. The salvation of every earthly father came through the Son of the eternal Father, and this Son saved man in conjunction with his earthly father. This signifies that a father's salvation is brought about in some manner by his own child, and that a child's salvation is brought about, in some manner, by his own father. By bringing a child into covenant with God, the father has accepted the task of becoming a living example of one whose life is solidly established in God's covenant with man, and in becoming this example for his child, he enables his child to bring him more deeply into covenant with God.

---

[207]   See Philippians 2:7

# DAY 44

INFLICTING THE WOUND: A PERPETUAL SIGN OF LOVE

Another reason for Joseph's fatherly presence during the circumcision is to demonstrate that the father, Joseph, initiated Jesus into God's covenant by inflicting a wound that served as a perpetual reminder to Jesus of his father's love for Him. Here love is signified by a wound inflicted by the lover upon the loved one. If a father loves his child, he must at some point introduce him to the ways of God, which are often painful. Hypothetically speaking, if Joseph had decided to recoil from his duty of inflicting Christ with the covenantal wound to spare his child from pain, the child would have been made subject to the dreadful pain of being outside of God's covenant. For the Lord said, "So shall my covenant be in your flesh as an everlasting sign."[208] Brother, see that God's ways are directly linked to discipline, "for the Lord disciplines him Whom He loves and chastises every son whom He receives."[209] Though this discipline of the covenant is placed in a child's flesh, we shall see that this initiation of the flesh must be transferred to the inner sprit of the child lest it be only an outer sign, lacking inner substance.

[208] Genesis 17:14
[209] Hebrews 12:6

### Baptism: The Initiation of the New Covenant

Though the marks of circumcision in a child's flesh serve as a perpetual reminder of his father's love, this mark is only etched into the outer image of the child, leaving an inner transformation to be sought. Baptism, by the mercy of God, is an outer sign of the inner reality of the indwelling of the Holy Spirit of God, thus marking God's love upon the inner soul of the child with the image of Christ. Circumcision, exclusively for the male child, gave way to baptism for all children. Circumcision was an outer sign of man's faithfulness to God; baptism is the inner reality of God's faithfulness to man. Circumcision deformed the body, but baptism transforms the body and spirit.

My brother, it is your duty as a father to grant your child access to the transforming Spirit of the Father, for baptism "is for you and your children and those who are far off,"[210] and it is most certainly prudent to grant your children access to baptism while they are yet children rather than before they become "far off." No father would be so imprudent as to deny his child food until the child is of age and capable of feeding himself. So it is with grace. A grace-filled father grants his child access to the Father's grace as soon as the child has been given over to his guardianship. By his initiation into the covenant of grace through baptism, the child becomes a type of Christ by virtue of his dependence upon his earthly father, who is a type of Joseph, who introduces Christ into the covenant with God the Father.

A father is to initiate his child into the sacrificial way of God by first drowning the sin of his child's flesh in the baptismal font and raising his child from the waters of death to new life. By doing this, the father is acknowledging that his primary allegiance or affection is not toward the child of his flesh, but to the child of God's Spirit.

---

[210]   Acts 2:39

Though baptism does not leave a perpetual mark of the father's love upon his child's flesh, it does leave an indelible mark upon the child's sprit, signifying that the child no longer belongs to his earthly father, but, by right, belongs solely to the heavenly Father. Again, by baptizing his child, the father admits that his child is not merely related to him by the flesh but also by the Spirit, and that the child is not merely of his own earthly lineage but of the family of God.

# DAY 45

The gift of a child, received by a father from the heavenly Father, must be given in return to the Heavenly Father, Who returns the child to its earthly father for a period of time. The gift of the child is, in a sense, on loan, a talent that the master has entrusted to His servant while He is away. It is a father's duty to return this talent of his child to the Master with more than what was originally received. Remember the parable of the talents, my dear brother, keeping the Lord's words ever present in your heart: "From him who has been given much, much is expected, but from him who has little, even what he has will be taken away."[211]

The talent we have received in our children is no small matter, but a life-long task entrusted to us and a deposit on which we must make a return. We must enter into the dynamic of the talent by receiving the talent, that is, the gift of the child, from God; giving back the child by means of a consecration to God; receiving the child in return from God to care for and nurture—or in keeping with the analogy, multiplying the talents—and then finally giving the child to God by giving the child the freedom to give his own life in submission to God.

As with fatherhood, baptism is often regarded superficially, in this case as a mere ritual, lacking any deep transformative significance. However, just as a profound ontological change occurs in the human person by means of baptism, so too when a father

---

[211]    See Matthew 13:12, 25:29

strives to increase the talent of his own child, he helps to achieve a significant transformation in the child.

You, child of the Heavenly Father, have been given much in the gift of your child, and you must acknowledge it as such, lest your ingratitude cause you to become slothful in your guardianship of the gift. By believing that you have been given much, your gratitude towards the Generous One will, most assuredly, inspire you to respond in generosity to the gift of your child and toward the Giver of the child. Our hope, as fathers, is one day to hear those most consoling words, "Well done my good and faithful servant. You have been faithful in small matters, I will give you greater responsibilities, come share your Master's joy."[212]

Though this matter of raising a child to holiness may appear to be a small matter from the perspective of many earthly fathers, it should be viewed by the servant as a great responsibility. Indeed, many fathers, if not a majority, fall into the error of viewing their own fatherhood as small - a little talent, which should be buried in comparison to their occupation, personal projects, or desired endeavors, which all seem more important than the side matter of raising a child to personal holiness.

Often, the matter that is small in the eyes of the inexperienced judgment of men is truly great in the eyes if God, for the reason that greater matters depend upon the smaller matter's fulfillment. Therefore, the task of training a child in the art of holy sacrifice is indeed a great matter.

Every father will be judged according to how he invested the talent of his child, and according to whether he returned the talent of the child to God, for the Lord said, "Consecrate to Me all the firstborn; whatever is the first to open the womb among the people

---

[212]   See Matthew 25:21

of Israel, both of man and beast is Mine."[213] We may also say that, by means of the new covenant, every child that opens the womb is His.

Joseph, understanding that Jesus, his new Son, was not of his own flesh, but belonged to God, "brought him up to Jerusalem to present him to the Lord...(as it is written, every male that opens the womb shall be called holy to the Lord),"[214] and so "the parents brought in the child Jesus, to do for Him according to the custom of the law."[215] Echoing God's command, the law demanded that a sacrifice be offered to the Lord for the child that opened the womb. This sacrifice served as the price of redemption of the child from the Lord. God received this sacrifice as a sign that the child was fully consecrated to Him, and, receiving the sign of consecration, He in turn gave the child back as a sign of His fidelity. This rite of redemption served as a reminder of the original Passover, when God spared the first born of all who were willing to consecrate themselves to Him by the act of sacrifice, and of all who perished for their unwillingness to sacrifice to God.[216]

Joseph, offering sacrifice to God, "redeemed" the One Who redeemed all by His own sacrifice; for what Jesus could not do as a babe Joseph was commanded "to do for Him."[217] See how dependent Jesus was, in His human state, upon his earthly father Joseph! The Lord Jesus allowed Himself to become dependent upon Joseph for His "redemption" according to the old covenant so that his father, and all fathers, might be redeemed by His "blood of the new and everlasting covenant."[218] The Heavenly Father allowed the earthly father, Joseph, to redeem the Redeemer, entrusting Joseph to prepare His Son to become the sacrificial lamb. The redemption of

---

213   Exodus 13:2

214   Luke 2:23

215   Luke 2:27

216   See Exodus 12; Exodus 13:14

217   Luke 2:27

218   See Mark 14:24

Christ by his father Joseph serves as a permanent model for fathers who are to consecrate their children to God, redeeming the child, by God's grace, in baptism. By doing this, the father, like Joseph, offers his child in sacrifice to God, preparing his own child to offer himself eventually in sacrifice. How sad it is to see so many fathers, by misuse of reason, neglecting to consecrate their child to God by means of baptism. If Christ, before the age of reason, chose to be dependent upon a father to consecrate him to God the Father, should not we as fathers allow our children to do the same? "Let the little children come to me and do not hinder them."[219]

In this mystery, commonly referred to as the Presentation of the Lord, occurred an exchange of trust between God the Father and the father Joseph. Joseph freely gave the Son Whom he had received to God the Father, trusting that God would return the child; and God, returning the child, entrusted Joseph to prepare God's only begotten Son to be returned one day as the sacrificial oblation on behalf of all mankind. Joseph's faithfulness to this exchange of trust is one of the many testimonies of his fidelity to grace. Joseph's fidelity to the interior life always led to an external expression of the grace he received. My brother, see what trust the Father has placed in His children to become holy fathers of the children given to them! He entrusts each of us with the child He claims as His own. Have confidence that God has entrusted you with the great work of redeeming your child with Christ's redemption, of consecrating your child in baptism, wherein the child is "sealed with the promised Holy Spirit, Who is the pledge of our inheritance, for a redemption of possession, for the praise of His glory."[220] By redeeming a child in the bath of baptism, wherein Christ's redemptive power is given, we are granting to God, Who has granted us possession of our own child for a time, eternal possession of our own child.

---

[219]    Matthew 19:14
[220]    Ephesians 1:14

Isaac claimed Abraham as his own father, and Abraham, in claiming Isaac as his own child, claimed his sacrifice as his own; yet both were the Lord's. Joseph received Jesus as his own child, and Jesus received Joseph as his own father, yet both understood that Jesus was the Heavenly Father's only begotten Son. Abraham claimed Isaac as his own, binding him to become a sacrifice to God, while Joseph, receiving Jesus as his own, set the child free to become the Holy and Living Sacrifice of God. The father Joseph claimed Christ for God the Father, an act that every father, by obligation, should perform for his own child.

# DAY 46

### THE SIGN OF SEPARATION:
### JOSEPH'S AND JESUS' UNITIVE SACRIFICE

Though baptism removes the effects of original sin, it does not prevent the inevitable separation of body and soul caused by death. Abraham received a sign of separation, in the command to sacrifice his son, that caused his heart much grief, yet Abraham had faith that God would raise his son from the dead. Likewise, Joseph received a sign of separation, in Simeon's prophetic words to Mary, that caused his heart great distress and which also called him to great faith.

Brother, we shall discover that the unitive characteristic of sacrificial discipleship ironically contains the element of separation between the father and the child. In other words, the very sacrifice that unites a father and child will also cause their separation. While it is true that Christ said "What God has joined together let no man separate,"[221] it is also true that God uses the separation caused by man's sin to unite men together in God. Inevitably, all relationships united by God must undergo a separation, caused either by death or by the call to live for Christ, before the persons involved are permanently reunited in eternity.

Let us recall, dear brother, that Abraham's soul, while rejoicing in the miraculous gift of his son, was pierced by God's command to sacrifice his son on the hill of Moriah. Like Abraham, Joseph, in the midst of rejoicing over the gift of his new son, received from

---

[221] Mark 10:9

Simeon the prophecy of his child's destiny: the prophecy of the sword of sorrow that would one day pierce the Immaculate Heart of Mary. As he listened to Simeon's words, Joseph realized that the prophecy spoke only of Mary's heart being pierced, while there was no mention of his own heart, indicating his absence during this painful event. The reality of this future separation between himself and Jesus and Mary must have, in that very moment, pierced Joseph through.

Joseph's mission as guardian of the Virgin and Child was intrinsically bound up with his essence as a man, and yet it was ordained by God that the God-given task to be the guardian of the holy family was to be taken away from Joseph before Christ's passion and death. How difficult this must have been for Joseph to accept! Although Joseph may not have known with certainty of the crucifixion and death of Jesus, he at the very least understood, in the depth of his being, that the future held unspeakable events which would affect both Jesus and his mother, as indicated by Simeon's prophecy.

Friend, as fathers, we are granted the privilege of protecting the family with our very lives, and yet we must embrace the possibility that we may not be ordained to protect them in their time of visitation. Considering this prospect, each father must depend entirely upon the grace of God to prepare his family for their heavenly home, which is paved with the stones of embraced sacrifices. The prophetic words of Simeon remind every father that separation is unavoidable, and rather than dwelling upon what the future may have in store, we must not waste any time, but use each moment to prepare our own children to become capable of sacrificing themselves for our God, even if our aid be absent. The future separation between the father and his family should not separate us from God's will, but rather serve as a means of uniting us with God. If a father prudently prepares his child for the separation that death will bring, this separation will ultimately end with the child and the father being reunited in Christ. If, however, the father misuses the time he has been given to prepare his child for this separation, the separation between the two may become permanent.

Throughout his life, the words of Simeon most certainly echoed in Joseph's soul, constantly reminding him of his duty to prepare the Virgin and the Christ to embrace the suffering which the future held, knowing that they would be without his presence and aid. As with Joseph, Simeon's words should be seared into our hearts, so that we may attentively use our talents to prepare our family for the narrow gate, that "thicket of suffering"[222] which truly is the only path to the eternal rapture.

Every father who tenderly loves his own child recognizes that life is fragile and will one day come to an end. Either the father will lose his child to earthly death, or the child will lose his father. Neither can escape death, for even Christ, the Son of God, did not spare Himself from death, but embraced it fully. Consideration of the fact of death may lead to thoughts of loneliness, worry, even doubt or despair; but all of these emotions prove to be useless unless they motivate us to give ourselves more to our children in the time they have been given to us.

---

[222]   St. John of the Cross, *Spiritual Canticle*

# DAY 47

Joseph first tasted this bitter separation during his second recorded trek to Jerusalem, when the twelve year old Jesus was initiated into spiritual adulthood by celebrating the Passover feast. Bringing Jesus to Jerusalem for the Passover, Joseph repeated through his actions the spoken words of Abraham: "I and the lad will go yonder and worship, and come again to you."[223] "They went both of them together";[224] "when He was twelve years old, they went up according to the custom."[225]

The custom referred to was, most certainly, the Passover feast wherein the Israelites, depending upon their fervor, went to a local synagogue or made the pilgrimage to the temple in Jerusalem, offering sacrifice to their God as a reminder of Israel's deliverance, by God's mighty hand, from slavery to Pharaoh. Reading this custom through the lens of Joseph's and Jesus' trek, we discover that the Passover custom was built upon Abraham's sacrifice of his son Isaac. The custom of the Passover, in which all of Israel was commanded by God to sacrifice a lamb as a reminder of the original Passover, originated with Abraham's trek up mount Moriah and his prophetic words, "God Himself will provide the Lamb."[226] Joseph and the young Jesus climbed the hill to Jerusalem, fulfilling the

---

[223] Genesis 22:5

[224] Genesis 22:8

[225] Luke 2:42

[226] Genesis 22:8

custom of sacrificing the paschal lamb, and also beginning the process of the ultimate fulfillment of the custom of Abraham's sacrificial offering of his son Isaac in the offering to God of the true paschal Lamb of God. By carrying out the traditional custom of sacrificing the paschal lamb, Joseph began the new custom of offering the true Paschal Lamb, and doing this, he began a new custom for every father; the offering of one's own child, with his child's consent, as another lamb of God. Brother, you are not only to initiate your child as an infant into God's covenant through baptism, but also to continue the custom of initiating your child into spiritual adulthood by presenting your child to God as one who is ready and willing to offer his life to God of his own accord.

Fulfilling the traditional custom of the Passover with his Son Jesus by initiating Him as an adult into the Jewish religious assembly, Joseph further initiated himself into the essence of fatherhood, the sacrifice of one's attachment to his child for the sake of attaching the child to God. This mutual penetration into each other's vocation, in direct pursuit of one's own vocation, is the essential characteristic of the unitive sacrifice of a father and a son. When a father initiates his child into spiritual adulthood, the father is accordingly moved deeper into his vocation as a father, for as the two fulfill this rite together, the expectancy and reality of separation becomes more evident. This truth is expressed eloquently in the sacrament of Confirmation where parents, with the full consent of the child, present their child to God and the Church, desiring that their child receive the spiritual seal of the Holy Spirit, which draws one from the world and empowers one to become a witness to the resurrected Christ.

In Baptism the first beam of the cross, the horizontal beam, is spiritually placed upon the child as the burden of love given by the Holy Spirit. The infant grows to understand that he has been given a great responsibility to share with others the charity which the Holy Spirit has given and which He prompts the individual in turn to give. This first beam of the cross was set upon the child by his parents at Baptism. In the sacrament of Confirmation the parents give the child permission to take up the second beam of the cross, the vertical beam of the sacrifice of self, which is united with the first beam, commending to the youth the task of faithfully carrying the entire cross himself. This second beam, the seal of the Spirit in Confirmation, separates the child from his parents, for he must give himself freely and of his own accord to God, who lifts him up from the world by his witness to Christ, thus drawing people from the world to Christ through him.

This consecration goes beyond baptism because it involves not only the will and intentions of the youth's parents, but also the will and intention of the youth. On the human level, the parents and the child together confirm their aspirations that the youth be set apart for God's service. On the spiritual level, the Holy Spirit chooses the youth and sets him apart, claiming him as one who is to be filled with his Holy breath, giving him the privileged duty to proclaim the Gospel message, while beginning the process of confirming the youth in a holy fire that purifies him like fire-tried gold, enabling him to become a profitable witness of Christ. This sacrament is unitive in that the parents, the youth, and the Holy Spirit in unison give consent to the child's entry into the life of the Holy Spirit, which is spiritual adulthood. This happens by means of the purification provided by the fire of the Holy Spirit, which is two-fold: first, the Holy fire purifies the youth of earthly attractions, giving him a spirit of adoption, empowering him to "suffer with Christ." Second, the Holy Fire purifies the parents' earthly attachment to their child, enabling them to heed Christ's words, "He who loves son or daughter more than me is not worthy of me."[227]

---

[227]    Matthew 10:37

Mingled with the unitive characteristic is an awareness of the separation that must occur between the parents and the youth, a separation that will allow the youth to embrace his particular vocation of his own accord, thus heeding Christ's words, "He who loves father or mother more than me is not worthy of me."[228]

More than a cultural rite or custom done for the sake of religious continuity, the rite of confirmation is a receiving of the life-giving Spirit Who is "no cowardly spirit,"[229] but a Spirit Who gives strength and courage, enabling the dead to love Life, but deterring one from loving life so much as to fear death.[230]

The separation that is induced between loved ones by the gift of the Holy Spirit should never separate one from God's will. Rather, this separation should serve as a means of uniting both the parents and the youth with God. Thus, even in their separation, the father and the child will be unified in their faith, offering their lives in unity for the holy cause. We cannot help but to recall the examples of many young men and women who, by means of the priesthood and religious life, entered the mission fields, were often distanced thousands of miles from their own families to bear witness to the resurrection of Christ, and who yet remained unified with their families by a spiritual bond of faith.

My brother, if this discussion of separation should cause you any anxiety or doubt, look to Joseph and his son Jesus who, after the Passover feast, became separated from one another. After three days of anxious searching, the parents of Jesus found him in the temple, asking Him, "Son, why hast Thou done so to us? Behold, in sorrow Thy father and I have been searching for Thee."[231] And He said to them, "How is it that you sought me? Did you not know that I

---

228    ibid

229    2 Timothy 1:7

230    See Revelation 12:17

231    Luke 2:48

must be about my father's business?"[232] Unlike Abraham, who heard the salutation of Isaac, "my Father," Joseph heard Jesus' words, "my Father's business." Perhaps, after meditating upon these mysterious words of Christ, Joseph reconciled himself with the reality that Jesus had identified Himself as the Son of the Heavenly Father, in a sense surpassing his identification with His earthly father. By accidentally abandoning his son, Joseph was forced to abandon himself to his son's Heavenly Father, discovering that he must also abandon his son to the Heavenly Father. Abandoning his son and himself to God the Father, Joseph was not abandoned by God or his son, for "He went down with him becoming subject to him."[233] Be assured, dear brother, that separation willed by God does not grant a child permission to separate disobediently from his father. Therefore, do not cling to your child, but release him at the proper time, so that he may become obedient to God the Father.

We may derive another valuable lesson from the unitive sacrifice of Joseph and the Child Jesus. It is quite possible that just as Abraham placed the burden of the wood of discipline upon Isaac, Joseph placed the lamb of sacrifice upon his son during Christ's first Passover. Beyond placing the wood of discipline upon his son, Joseph placed the burden of sacrifice upon Jesus. As his father began to place the lamb upon Christ's shoulders, Jesus fixed His gaze upon the lamb of sacrifice, seeing, as in an allegorical mirror, an image of himself, yet an image that in itself was unable to satisfy the demands of the law. Likewise, Christ became man, taking upon Himself the image of man whose ransom for his own life was beyond him. The Lamb of God carried the lamb of sacrifice, foreshadowing the day when the Man-God carried mankind to Calvary. In Christ, Man carried himself, to sacrifice Himself for all of mankind. The lamb placed by Joseph upon the Lamb is an

---

[232]   Luke 2:49
[233]   Luke 2:51

example for fathers, calling each of us to place the burden of self-sacrifice upon the child, encouraging the child to become another "sheep led to the slaughter"[234] to "make up for what is lacking in the suffering of Christ's body."[235]

My brother, these words direct us to live in the present time, savoring each moment as a means of preparing our children for their future sacrifice. We must be careful not to stray off into the unreal, unknown future, for if we do we will miss the present opportunity to lead them to Christ. Yet if we wholly immerse ourselves in the present time, we deny the necessity of preparing for the reality of our child's future. Rather than enjoying the present without preparing for the child's future, we must live in the reality of the present time while making a child's future self-sacrifice a reality.

---

[234]   See Romans 8:36

[235]   Colossians 1:24

# DAY 48

## The Vicarious Stage of Fatherly Sacrifice

Isaac spoke to his father Abraham, saying, "Behold, the fire and the wood; but where is the lamb for a burnt offering?" Abraham said, "God will provide Himself the Lamb for a burnt offering my son."[236] Once again, by calling Isaac "my son," Abraham embraced his son as his own, while also claiming Isaac's sacrifice as his own. "So they went both of them together" to sacrifice to the Lord, and together they were one sacrifice.

The third stage of sacrificial discipleship is vicarious in nature. After much preparation, a father must confront the reality that he does not have the right to perform his child's sacrifice himself. Rather, the father must release his child, allowing the child to decide freely whether or not he is to become a holy and living sacrifice unto the Lord. This freedom is essential to the sacrifice of the child, for every human being is created for his own sake. Despite the goodness of the intention, a father should not force his children to sacrifice their own will for the will of God. If the child chooses the path of self-sacrifice, the father must recognize that the sacrifice is his child's, and yet also recognize that he is living vicariously through his child's sacrifice. As we have said, a father is called to walk the way of sacrifice with his son. By going together to sacrifice to the Lord, the two are one in sacrifice, though in the end a person can only sacrifice himself.

---

[236] Genesis 22:7-8

The first element of a vicarious sacrifice is the sacrifice of the child must be freely chosen by the child and not mandated by the father. In other words, the father relinquishes all control over his child's sacrificial path. The second element is that the father sacrifices himself precisely by relinquishing control over his child's sacrifice, and that therefore his child's sacrifice becomes his own. The father sacrifices himself through his child by preparing his child for sacrifice, while the child sacrifices himself to the heavenly Father with all that his earthly father has given him. This is what is meant by the father vicariously sacrificing himself through his own child.

Brother, in case any clarification needs to be made, this does not mean that fathers are to determine how or in what manner their child is to become "a holy and living sacrifice unto the Lord,"[237] nor does this mean that the father has any right to coerce his child to become a sacrificial offering. Either by determining a particular path of sacrificial offering, or by pressing his child into embarking upon the way of the cross by means of an imposed vocation, the father has not allowed the child to choose self-sacrifice freely, but rather has denied the child the opportunity to give himself freely to the Lord. A father who does such a thing has made no sacrifice of his own, for he has not sacrificed his longing to control his child, nor has he submitted his vicarious longings to the will of God the Father, Who truly lived vicariously through the free will of His Son.

Indeed, due to the reality of free will, a child who has become mature enough to decide for or against God may rebel and desire not to desire to live for God. This also serves, even more painfully, as a form of separation between a faithful father and an unfaithful child. The father must accept the decision of the child to rebel against God, but must never refrain from sacrificing to God and praying that the child will return to God. Though this type of

---

[237]   Romans 12:1

separation can be a reality, history demonstrates that most children of faithful fathers will remain faithful to their Father in heaven.

The vicarious sacrifice of a father through his child is forged in the many years of foundational preparation wherein a father spends himself tirelessly, pouring himself into his child, teaching the child the secrets of self-sacrifice. The father understands that he is only capable of preparing his child for sacrifice, planting within his child seeds of a self-offering that may one day "fall to the ground to bear much fruit."[238] A father is to walk the road of sacrifice with his child, not walk the path for his child; he is to encourage the child to complete the way of the cross, without carrying the cross for him. For this sacrifice of the father to be truly vicarious, meaning that the sacrifice is lived out through his own child, he must sacrifice any of his own personal aspirations that he may desire to be lived out through his own child, save that of obedience to the will of God through the sacrifice of self. This sacrifice of a father's personal desires becomes the sacrifice that is passed on and carried out vicariously through the father's own child. In other words, if a father desires to live unfulfilled dreams vicariously through his own child, he has denied the essence of the vicarious sacrifice, which is the sacrifice of a father's self-will in exchange for God the Father's will.

Keep in the forefront of your mind, dear friend, that a father is only to prepare, guide, and encourage, never to mandate a particular path or vocation for his child. If the father's sacrifice of his child is to be truly vicarious, he must submit his own will to the will of God Who decides how the child is to be sacrificed.

---

[238] John 12:24

# DAY 49

ABRAHAM: THE VICARIOUS STAGE
OF FATHERLY SACRIFICE

Though Abraham was obedient to God's command to sacrifice his son, his sacrifice was not entirely vicarious, for he bound Isaac against the child's free will. The fact that Abraham bound Isaac leads us to believe that Isaac was not completely resigned to offer himself freely in sacrifice. By binding Isaac, Abraham did not remain bound by the vicarious nature of the sacrifice. Additionally, God did not allow Abraham to sacrifice his son, for the son was not allowing himself to be given, and God did not force Isaac to become a sacrifice that he was not willing to be. Brother, God only receives a gift of self-sacrifice from one who willingly receives the gift of being sacrificed from the One Who has sacrificed Himself for all. God wills that one use free will to give his own will freely to the One true God. In his obedience Abraham did not withhold his son from God, and yet God withheld his acceptance of Abraham's son given in obedience. Why would God do such a thing? Brother, one of the reasons may be that God has demonstrated to us that no father, not even a father under the command of God, is authorized by God to force his child, against his own will, to become a sacrificial lamb, "for God Himself will provide the Lamb."[239]

Here we recall, dear brother, the account of Jepthah, who made a vow to the Lord: "Whoever comes forth from the doors of my house to meet me, when I return victorious from the Ammonites,

---

[239]   Genesis 22:8

shall be the LORD's, and I will offer him up for a burnt offering."[240] After Jephtah smote the Ammonites, he came to his home,

> and behold, his daughter came out to meet him with timbrels and with dances; she was his only child; beside her he had neither son nor daughter. And when he saw her, he rent his clothes, and said, "Alas, my daughter! You have brought me very low, and you have become the cause of great trouble to me; for I have opened my mouth to the LORD, and I cannot take back my vow.[241]

Our concern is not with Jepthah and his personal vow to the Lord, but rather the response of his daughter. At first glance, we may suppose that the Lord demanded that Jepthah sacrifice his daughter against her own will, but let us examine her response: "My father, if you have opened your mouth to the LORD, do to me according to what has gone forth from your mouth."[242]

What can we discern from these haunting accounts? Though Abraham was ordained by God to sacrifice Isaac, he constrained Isaac, which indicates that their sacrifice was at some level against Isaac's free will. This implies that the act of worship offered to God by the father Abraham, and Isaac the son, was lacking the unitive quality.

Conversely, Jepthah, vowed to the Lord to make such a sacrifice without God ordaining him to do so—yet his daughter complied with her father's vow so as not to make him sin. Indeed, she freely surrendered herself in sacrifice, expressing, in herself, the character of unitive sacrifice. However, Jepthah failed as a father, for he sacrificed that which only God should sacrifice, which indicates that the sacrifice of Jepthah and his daughter was not completely unitive.

---

[240] Judges 11: 31
[241] Judges 11:34-35
[242] Judges 11:36

Indeed, my brother, God alone can sacrifice His own Son, precisely because God is the Son Who wished to offer Himself in sacrifice to the Father; for "God Himself will provide the Lamb,"[243] that is, God alone can provide the sacrificial Son.

If Jesus had been unwilling to comply to the Father's desire for Him to be sacrificed, the offering of the Father and the Son would have lacked the unitive characteristic. True filial worship, that is, worship offered by both a father and his child, must always contain within itself the unitive characteristic.

If Jepthah had chosen to fulfill the will of God, he would have done what God later did, namely sacrificing himself with his child. God the Father sacrificed Himself in His Son, in place of us, His adopted children.

On the one hand, Abraham was obedient, and yet Isaac's gift of self was lacking. On the other hand, Jepthah's daughter sacrificed herself freely, and yet Jepthah did not sacrifice himself. Both of these offerings lack the ideal character of unitive sacrifice.

As we will see, my brother, where Abraham and Jepthah fail, Joseph succeeds in that he offered himself in unity with Christ for the sake of humanity. Joseph did not coerce or force Jesus to make His thanksgiving sacrifice. Nor did he attempt to constrain Jesus or His future by detaining Him for his own benefit. Indeed, Joseph, like so many fathers of our present age, could have succumbed to the temptation to use his child for his own gain, or to neglect his child, or even to attempt to deter the Son of God from His divine mission to save mankind.

Joseph, however, unified himself with the Father's plan to prepare Jesus for His own sacrifice—without accomplishing it for Jesus. In this manner Joseph unified himself with the sacrifice of Christ.

---

[243] Genesis 2:28

Perhaps, my brother, we should concern ourselves with Jepthah and his personal vow to the Lord. The question must be raised: under what pretext did Jepthah make a vow to sacrifice a member of his family or one of his servants? Was it justifiable for Jepthah to promise to sacrifice a human being, particularly a member of his family, in exchange for victory over the Ammonites? The princes of Galaad had promised Jepthah that if he would fight the Ammonites he would rule as prince over them. This reward lured Jepthah into valuing conquest and honor among men over the hidden victories accomplished in familial life.

In other words, Jepthah valued himself, his honor, his achievements, the respect of men and the power that men give, over his family. In fact, to make such a vow indicates that Jepthah subjectively understood the human person, particularly his family members, as objects who were at his disposal. The human person, however, is not the type of being that is to ever be used. "Therefore Jepthah's action cannot be justified."[244]

Jepthah's example stands as the antithesis of a true father who sacrifices himself, and his desire for honor, power, and the respect of men in exchange for his family. Indeed, God sacrifices Himself for the sake of His family, and as we will see, Joseph, as icon and imitator of the Father, also sacrificed himself in hiddenness and self-sacrificial service in order that Jesus and Mary might thrive.

---

[244]   *The Navarre Bible, Joshua-Kings*, page 157

# DAY 50

Joseph, likewise, was granted the incredible task of preparing the Son of God to become the Lamb of God Who takes away the sins of the world. Joseph's Son, however, was completely willing to ascend the mount of Calvary with the wood of discipline upon his back. The fundamental difference between Abraham and Joseph is that Abraham bound his son to become the sacrificial offering, whereas Joseph was bound by his very vocation to offer his son, who willingly offers Himself as the sacrificial offering. A father is not to sacrifice his son but to sacrifice himself through the sacrifice of his own son. Fulfilling this task is Joseph's personal gift over and above Abraham.

Although Joseph faithfully fulfilled the task of preparing Jesus for His self oblation, Joseph was not afforded the opportunity to journey a third time up the hill to Jerusalem where His Son handed Himself over to be scourged, mocked, and crucified. Dear brother, we must be completely resigned to train our children willingly in the ways of self-sacrifice, regardless of whether or not we will be given the gift of being present on their day of offering. Many of us will not be rewarded with seeing the destiny of our children, but, like Joseph, we must dedicate ourselves to doing all that grace allows us in preparing each child for his own personal Calvary.

*Conclusion*

# DAY 51

## GOD PROVIDES THE SACRIFICE

My brother, both Joseph and Abraham demonstrated great faith by believing without seeing, and both were rewarded according to their faith in God. The reward, however, that God gave them for their wholehearted trust, was the mission to willingly to give their heir to God in sacrifice. Yet God did not demand that Abraham and Joseph sacrifice their sons directly, but rather in a vicarious manner. Abraham attempted to sacrifice a son who was not willing to be sacrificed, whereas Joseph sacrificed himself for a Son Who was willing to be sacrificed.

God, however, did not allow Abraham to sacrifice his son, nor did God allow Joseph to see his son sacrificed. God alone has the right to sacrifice His own Son and be with His Son throughout His sacrificial offering, for He is fully one with His own Son. The heavenly Father did not force Jesus to sacrifice Himself, nor did the Son coerce the Father to sacrifice the Son. United as one God, *God provided the Lamb* of sacrifice, for the Lamb was God. From this fact we discover a great truth in regards to the mysterious, vicarious sacrifice of a father through his child: A father reveals himself, though he remains hidden, through the sacrifice of his own child. The Heavenly Father has revealed Himself through His Son Jesus Christ's incarnation, life, death, and resurrection. By means of the incarnation, leading to the crucifixion, the Son reveals the Father, and by means of the resurrection, the Father reveals the Son. God the Father's fatherhood is entirely unique in that He has been revealed by His Son because He and His son are one. We as fathers do not have the right to sacrifice our own children, for we are not fully one with them. In other words, every child must reveal something about himself, and this revelation of self is unveiled through the sacrifice of self: "man only finds himself by becoming a sincere gift."[245] God the Father had the right to sacrifice His Son because His Son was His own revelation of self. Every father, however, is in some way revealed by the sacrifice of his own child, for "the Lord honors the father in his children."[246]

My brother, you need not concern yourself with offering your child in sacrifice, for "God Himself will provide the lamb."[247] If God wills that your child become a sacrificial lamb in union with the Lamb of Sacrifice, trust that God will provide, "for on the mount it will be provided."[248] Our concern is not to prepare ourselves to sacrifice our child, but to prepare our child for self-sacrifice. By placing the wood of discipline, the cross, upon His own Son, leading him up Calvary, and there sacrificing Him on behalf of each of us, God fulfills the demands of the law, carrying out justice upon Himself, enabling each of us who could not fulfill the law in our fatherhood to fulfill the law of love by mercifully sacrificing our own desires in exchange for the desires of God the Father. A father's self-identity and self-sacrifice is ultimately revealed in the self-sacrifice of his child, but can also be revealed in his unfailing love toward the prodigal child who remains in rebellion; for both expressions of fatherhood are essentially found in God the Father, who is identified and revealed in the sacrament of His own Son, but Whose love is also revealed by loving those children who have failed in loving Him. This is the great genius of fatherhood.

---

[245]  *Gaudium et Spes* 24

[246]  Sir 3:2

[247]  ibid

[248]  Genesis 22:14

Let us, dear brother, imitate the silent action of Joseph, expressing deep faith in Almighty God, Who promises in Christ that our children will be among those more numerous than the stars. To follow this model of Joseph's prayer of faith is to pray earnestly for the justice of the kingdom, a justice that God brings to fruition through fathers who offer their children as willing sacrifices. My friend, Joseph's example is a deep well of faith, obedience, and sacrifice from which all fathers should drink. Through Christ and His life Joseph has been revealed, and it is from our very own offspring that we fathers will become known, and that Christ will be known in us.

PRAYER OF PERSEVERANCE –
# A PRAYER OF HOPE

# DAY 52

## THE HOPE OF A FATHER

Now that you are aware of your God-given mission to offer your child in sacrifice to the Heavenly Father, obstacles, trials, and hindrances of various kinds will arise. Indeed, you may suffer intense temptations to flee from this narrow and rocky path. But for you, dear father, who have been chosen by God the Father to be a father, there is no other path to sanctity besides marriage and no other road to holiness than fatherhood.

Be not entertained with the illusion that this mission has not been specifically granted to you, that this mission is not worthy of you, that you are not worthy of this mission, or that fatherhood is reserved for only certain pious individuals, or for those who appear to have no special piety. This is not the case. The greatness of fatherhood is offered to all fathers who are willing to cooperate with God's redemptive grace.

By nature of the office of holy fatherhood, the demand to offer your children in sacrifice has been laid upon you, but also offered to you is the grace necessary to fulfill this holy work. To cooperate with God in forming your child into a temple of the Holy Spirit, as an offering holy and pleasing to God, it is vital that you build your domestic church. For a child to become a temple of God, the child should dwell in a godly temple. The domestic church is a prototype of the divine sanctuary wherein the Triune God dwells.

The primary purpose of this earthly sanctuary is to become a link that connects the child with his heavenly homeland. If a child would one day live in heaven, heaven must live on earth

today. Therefore the holy domestic church, which God is building
through you, must become a living, breathing icon of the most holy
Triune God. God created the family to be a symbol of the exchange
of persons of the Trinity, and the purpose of this icon is to provide
mankind with a link between heaven and earth, a reminder of our
destiny which inspires a new hope in the joy that awaits us in the
Fatherland. Brother, this is your mission; this is your blessing; this
is your cross.

Be not afraid of this cross, for it is your path to holiness. If a
man is to be drawn by divine gravity like the drop of water into the
chalice of wine, or in other words, if he is to be drawn by God into
the eternal bliss and rapture of the divine exchange of love, he must
be drawn through that narrow gate, the "thicket of suffering."[249]
This is precisely the truth we profess when we sign ourselves
with the cross. In essence, we are saying, "I proclaim, profess and
acknowledge that I desire to be drawn by divine gravity into the
eternal exchange of love, to be permeated completely by the divine
wine of love, and to swim in self-giving love for all eternity. Yet I
also acknowledge that I can only enter into the eternal exchange of
love by means of the narrow gate, the thicket of suffering, the cross
that You, O God, have intended for me from all eternity. Lord have
mercy on me, that I may persevere to the end and be saved!"

Fatherhood is a blessing that also contains a curse. Indeed, every
blessing is associated with a curse. Consider the Blessed Mother,
whose greatest blessing was her Son, the Son of the Most High. Yet
the great blessing of Jesus was accompanied by the terrible scourge
of the crucifixion. This dynamic is also true for each and every
father whose wife and children are among his greatest gifts, but
also, in some sense, are the crosses which help to purify his soul.
Indeed, it is precisely by means of living in relationship with his
wife and children that a father will undergo countless humiliations,

---

[249]  St. John of the Cross, *Spiritual Canticle*

which if embraced, will afford humility, the foundation of the domestic church.

Heedless of this cross, we must persevere in faith, setting our sights upon the goal of building the domestic church. Indeed, the first of the four pillars of a father's prayer life is the "Prayer of Faith," and the second pillar, which builds upon it, is the "Prayer of Perseverance," also known as the prayer of hope. Perseverance presupposes a pre-existing hope. Without something hoped for we lack perseverance, but if we truly hope for something we are more likely to persevere in order to attain it. We must hope to persevere and persevere in hope to achieve the lofty yet attainable goal of bringing the Fatherland to earth so that our children may one day dwell in the eternal Fatherland of heaven. This lofty goal can be accomplished by building the domestic sanctuary, not with stones and mortar, but with humility, fortitude and a willingness to allow God to transform us into who we have been created to be.

We, dear brother, cannot afford to live a life of faith without perseverance. Faith without perseverance is not faith at all, but a counterfeit. A man lacking perseverance is one who "holds the form of religion but denies the power of it."[250] Faith without perseverance is faith without hope. Building upon this understanding that perseverance is essential in fulfilling our endeavor, we must learn what the prayer of perseverance is, what it demands, and the goal toward which it presses.

---

[250]   See 2 Timothy 3:5

# DAY 53

THE THREE ELEMENTS OF THE
PRAYER OF PERSEVERANCE

The Prayer of Perseverance is composed of three elements: first, the reception of humility by means of humiliations, which will afford a man the humility necessary to wrestle with God. Wrestling with God, the second component of the Prayer of Perseverance, provides the context for a man to exercise and grow in fortitude, which is necessary for him not only to become the man that God created him to be, but also accomplish the third component of the Prayer of Perseverance, which is the firm establishment of his domestic church.

Many men, if not all, throughout their short lives, will encounter humiliation upon humiliation. In fact, it seems that many spend their lives strategizing and ordering their activities so as to avoid humiliations. By probing this experience we discover that beneath the desire to avoid humiliation is a deeper desire not to face our own limitations, or worse yet, our faults and sins. Often, to cope with our limitations, we hide our most frightening characteristics, especially our sinful past, consequently hiding our authentic self–even the good self–from others. In our efforts to hide the reality of who we are, we not only hide from our self but also hide ourselves from God, believing that we are who we think we are rather than who God knows us to be.

The key to overcoming humiliations is to reconcile our past, even and most especially our sinful past, with God, and from Him to receive the healing necessary to lead others, particularly our family, to holiness. If we choose to suppress the reality of the sinful past, even attempting to hide our sinfulness from God, the habits developed from such sins will continue to plague our own lives and the people with whom are involved. This has tragic results.

Both the unjust man whose habitual disposition is taking from others, and the just man, who strives to be a gift to others, will suffer humiliations. Yet the trajectory of their lives is different, based on their response to such humiliations.

Often the user and grasper resists and denies the humiliation, and in doing so he rejects the grace that is necessary to reconcile with God and even to reconcile with himself. By resisting humiliations a man continues to sink ever more deeply into his own personal quicksand of objectifying and grasping.

The just man, by means of receiving humiliations, accepts his own limitedness, embraces humility, and arises in fortitude, ultimately reconciling his past with God, and even himself.

The second element, known as "wrestling with God," consists of overcoming our internal resistance to God's pre-ordained plan for us. By breaking down these walls of resistance we exercise the divine virtue of fortitude, the substantial expression of humility, man's interior strength. These two sister virtues, humility and fortitude, are expressed in a firm resolution to obtain the hoped-for erection of the domestic sanctuary, which can succeed only with the merciful assistance of the Divine Architect. By means of a renewed understanding of self and confidence, which rests in God, a father becomes capable of leading his family to holiness by creating an environment that encourages the pursuit of holiness.

If we wish to build the domestic church, we must become leaders who embrace our call to greatness. Being unworthy of this call, as we all are, we achieve this greatness by means of humility and fortitude. In other words, we must first become followers of God to lead others effectively to God. Only by reconciling ourselves and our past with God can we begin to build the environment worthy of training our children for self-sacrifice. Otherwise, the tide of our deep-seated habits of using others for selfish gain will ripple out into our marriages and families.

Continuing with the methodology used in the previous letter, we will gain a clearer understanding of perseverance by comparing St. Joseph with his Old Testament pre-figuring type, the holy patriarch, Jacob. The holy fathers of antiquity together comprise a foreshadowing of St. Joseph, and Jacob provides a portion of this foreshadowing. With God's help, we will gather the life of Jacob, his desire for greatness, his humiliations, his acts of fortitude, his reconciliations, and synthesize these events with their symbolic character, comparing and contrasting them with a portion of Joseph's life and character, which is the model of perseverance for all fathers. Entering into this typological comparison will provide a valuable model of perseverance that is directly applicable to our vocation of fatherhood.

*Humility*

# DAY 54

## THE THREE COMPONENTS OF HUMILITY

Receiving humiliations, and learning from the lesson that God is teaching within such moments, run contrary to the fallen nature of man. The vice of pride, so deeply rooted in human beings, instinctively resists not only the humiliation, but also the idea that humiliations should be received and learned from. Humility is composed of three elements: first, man's proper direction of his desire for greatness, which can be used to glorify God or misused to glorify self as a god. The second component of humility is the proper response to humiliations when man's ego is pierced by a humiliation; this moment can prove to be a decisive turning point in a man's spiritual journey. How a man responds to humiliations indicates who he is desiring to glorify. Indeed it is a moment that is loaded with explosive power that, if harnessed, can launch a man into glory, but, if not reigned in, can destroy his life. The combination of the desire for greatness and the ability to receive humiliations is the third component: this integration of these two components yields humility, which is the foundation of all virtues and the basis of a life that is full of glory.

## Desire for Greatness

Burning within the carnal heart of man is a divine spark: the inspired desire for greatness. This desire, which is of divine origin, should motivate man from the depth of his being to break free from the captive chains of self and burst forth, in the name of God, to reveal the divine image to mankind. The desire for greatness is actuated by the desire to glorify the Glorious One. This longing for greatness is partially fulfilled by participating in the King's project to make the Kingdom great on earth, but is ultimately fulfilled by achieving eternal union with the great God.

The desire for greatness, welling up within man, rightly creates great ambitions to glorify God, through, with, and in the human person. The dignity of the human being can be summarized as this: being glorified by God by glorifying God. This dignity is a complete, gratuitous gift given by the Creator to the creature who responds by trusting and believing in the utter goodness of the gift; believing that "God will perfect the good work He has begun in him."[251]

Yet, quite often, we struggle with the difficulty of reconciling our desire for glory with the mysterious manner that God, in His divine wisdom, has chosen to bring that desire to fruition. Often man lacks patience in his effort to reconcile his desire for greatness with God's divine will, convincing himself to take control of the situation by relying solely upon his own powers and resources. By acting in this imprudent manner he thwarts the necessary purification of his inordinate desire for greatness, which would have transformed his soul to become receptive to the greatness and glory that only God can offer.

God invites each of us to embrace a period, or periods, of waiting, which serve to purify our eagerness for greatness, and also challenges us to reconcile our pursuit for greatness with our littleness. This is accomplished through a period of retreat, where we enter more deeply into conversation with God, distinguishing the impure motives of self-glorification from the pure motive of glorifying the Lord. Waiting upon His hand to direct us, He transforms those selfish motives into holy desires to glorify the selfless Christ, or

---

[251]  See Philippians 1:6

rather to be an expression of the glory of God in Christ. By actively, not passively, resting in this period of waiting, we will grant God permission to transform those impetuous presumptions of vain ambition and self-glory into His own desires.

During this period of waiting we will discover how dependent we are upon God to replace our self-exaltedness with humility, to cast off the cloak of self-deceit and discover the joy of our littleness. Indeed, "The Lord lifteth up all that fall: and setteth up all that are cast down,"[252] meaning that the Lord grants greatness and glory to those who cast themselves down in humility before God.

Indeed, it is true that the desire for greatness is a gift intended to propel man into union with the eternal God, but beware my friend, lest this desire become inverted, self-seeking, and tainted with impure motives and egocentric ambitions. The desire for greatness can consume a man like a metastasizing cancer, reducing him to a black-hole of self, which steals the life from those around him. Again, the desire for greatness is of divine origin, but can only genuinely be fulfilled by living solely for the God Who is our ultimate end. Often, man turns to the means rather than the end. He turns to his interior self where the desire for greatness lives, only to take up residence in the darkened cave of self, believing that this desire is his own possession.

Within you, fellow father, God has planted the divine desire for greatness. If you listen carefully, you will discover this desire beating like a battle drum within you. As you become more acquainted with this desire, you will discover a great tension that exists between the longing for the dream to be fulfilled and the patience demanded to attain it. God calls you to live in this tension, for it is within this tension that He is accomplishing your sanctification. But this will only be accomplished if you train yourself to wait upon the Lord and respond to His promptings accordingly.

---

[252]   Psalm 145:14

Be careful not to be ensnared by the belief that the Lord will accomplish your desire for greatness without your participation: this is sloth. Nor should you become anxious, taking matters into your own hands, pursuing paths that have not been marked out for you; this is presumption. Presumption causes man great turmoil, heartache, anxiety, and even despair, and can entice him to pursue greatness with methods full of selfish ambition, causing grief to himself and those around him. This can happen even if these methods appear to have the exterior mark of Christian character.

Remember that the desire for greatness is only great insofar as the desire is for the Great One. How often has the gift of desire become confused with the Giver of the desire, prompting a man to idolize the gift as a god rather than the God who gave the gift?

You, my fellow father, are called to greatness primarily within your own vocation of fatherhood. This is your primary means to greatness, and also God's tool for purifying your inordinate desire for greatness. Recall that the path to greatness begins with humility, and that leading your family to holiness is your path to holiness. By leading your family you will be following the Lord, and by following the Lord you will learn to be a leader worth following.

Let us first turn to the patriarch Jacob and compare his desire for greatness to that of Joseph, and by doing so, discover the path that leads to humility.

# DAY 55

## THE DESIRE OF JACOB

Within the soul of Jacob, son of Isaac, burned an intense desire for greatness. The Holy Scriptures reveal to us that this desire was programmed into his being by the God Who formed him within his mother's womb. Indeed, within Rebekah,

> The children struggled together ... and she said, "if it is thus, why do I live?" So she went to inquire of the Lord. And the Lord said to her, "Two nations are in your womb, and two peoples, born of you, shall be divided; the one shall be stronger than the other, the elder shall serve the younger.[253]

Jacob, the younger of the twins, was destined by God to rule Esau, his elder brother, and his lineage.

So instinctive was Jacob's desire for greatness that on the day of his birth he "came forth, and his hand had taken hold of Esau's heel; so his name was Jacob,"[254] meaning "he supplants."

As Jacob matured and aged, his desire for glory intensified, influencing his thoughts and behaviors. This desire for glory was so pervasive that,

> when Jacob was boiling pottage, Esau came in from the field, and he was famished. And Esau said to Jacob, "let me eat some of that

---

[253] Genesis 25:22-26
[254] Genesis 25:26

red pottage, for I am famished!" Jacob said, "First sell me your
birthright." Esau said, "I am about to die; of what use is a birthright to me?" Jacob said, "Swear to me first." So he swore to him
and sold his birthright to Jacob. Then Jacob gave Esau bread and
pottage of lentils, and he ate and drank, and rose and went his way.
Thus Esau despised his birthright.[255]

Jacob dealt shrewdly with Esau by taking from Esau's care what
Esau did not care for. It seems that Esau's lack of respect for his
birthright gave Jacob an implicit right to obtain it for his own. Yet
it also seems that Jacob exploited his brother's needs, taking advantage of Esau's weakened state to obtain the greatness he desired.

Despite Jacob's apparent tendency toward grasping, his shrewd-
ness proved to be divine prudence, for the pottage symbolized the
provision for the flesh, while the birthright symbolized the spiritual
gifts of God. Though Esau was skilled in the flesh and favored by
his father Isaac, Jacob was a man who sought after the gifts of God
and therefore was favored by the Heavenly Father.

Jacob's desire for greatness was the holy calling of God,
resounding within his being, inspiring him to seek after the Living
God. It was the Living God Who led the famished Esau into the
hands of Jacob. From this event, Jacob should have learned the valuable lesson that God can do all things and nothing is impossible for
Him,[256] for He can even convince a man to trade his birthright for
a bowl of lintel pottage.

Indeed, God afforded Jacob the opportunity to seize his brother's birthright in a just manner, and Jacob responded prudently by
seizing the opportunity. This event affords insight into the relationship God has with his people: He provides every opportunity for
glory, and we are to provide the response.

---

[255]   Genesis 25: 29-34
[256]   See Philippians 4:13

This lesson, however, was quickly erased from the mind of Jacob, for the desire of spiritual gifts is often not enough for one who lacks love, and exploits people. Even when gifts are perfect and have the potential to perfect the one who receives them, if such a person lacks love, the gifts amount to nothing,[257] unable to transform him. Jacob appeared to value the divine blessing, and yet apparently did not love God enough to love his brother.

Originally, Jacob desired greatness from the Great One, but this desire proved not to be the desire to love Love, but rather to love self above loving God. Indeed, the desire for greatness consumed Jacob, inducing him to use methods of trickery and guile, while casting off fidelity and honor to obtain his own glory. Rather than waiting upon divine providence to grant him a just means to achieve greatness, Jacob took matters into his own hands, relying upon his own resourcefulness to obtain the great blessing of his fathers. This act demonstrated Jacob's doubt that God could fulfill, in a just manner, the life-long desire of his heart. Indeed this act was Jacob's statement that guile is more effective than the ways of the just.

Jacob however, was not the only one who was guilty of guile, for it was his mother Rebekah who urged Jacob to trick his blind father Isaac into giving him the blessing by disguising himself as Esau.

Rebekah said to her son Jacob, "I heard your father speak to your brother Esau, 'bring me game, and prepare for me savory food, that I may eat it, and bless you before the Lord before I die.' Now therefore, my son, obey my word as I command you. Go to the flock, and fetch me two good kids, that I may prepare from them savory food for your father, such he loves; and you shall bring it to your father to eat, so that he may bless you before he dies." But Jacob said to Rebekah his mother, "Behold, my brother Esau is a

---

[257]    See 1 Corinthians 13:1-3

hairy man, and I am a smooth man. Perhaps my father will feel
me, and I shall seem to be mocking him, and bring a curse upon
myself and not a blessing." His mother said to him, "Upon me be
your curse, my son; only obey my word, and go, fetch them to me."
So he went and took them and brought them to his mother; and
his mother prepared savory food, such as his father loved. Then
Rebekah took the best garments of Esau her older son, which were
with her in the house, and put them on Jacob her younger son; and
the skins of the kids she put upon his hands and upon the smooth
part of his neck; and she gave the savory food and the bread, which
she had prepared, into the hand of her son Jacob."[258]

Notice, my brother, the apparent division between Isaac and
Rebekah, if not an outright dissent on Rebekah's part. Like Eve
who manipulated Adam into eating the forbidden fruit, so also
Rebekah resorted to the manipulation of Isaac to obtain what she
desired. It is imperative that we understand that such manipula-
tive behaviors are often transmitted from mother to child, and if
the child is male, such manipulation will emasculate him to some
degree. Division between a husband and wife often leads to the
emasculation of the male child.

My brother, keep this in mind as you proceed to build your
domestic church: if a house is divided it will not stand. As we will
see, the division between Rebekah and Isaac and her encouragement of Jacob to deceive his father inevitably led to the splintering
of their family. If a husband and wife do not stand as a united front,
the family will be susceptible to division, separation and chaos.

Jacob approached his blind father "and said, 'My father.'"[259]
Notice that Jacob echoes the same words his father Isaac spoke to his
father Abraham when carrying the wood upon his back to Mount

---

[258]   Genesis 21:6-17
[259]   Genesis 27:18

Moriah. Isaac said "My father," expressing a trustful surrender of self to his father, while Jacob said "My father," disguising a deceitful deed with the beautiful sound of self-surrender in order to make his father surrender what Jacob had desired. Jacob continued this deception by responding to his father's question, "Who are you, my son?", with the words, "I am Esau thy first-born."[260]

Again, Isaac's words have great meaning, for they are more than questioning Jacob's identity, but also questioning whether or not he is truly Isaac's son. In other words, Isaac senses that something is amiss and questions whether the one who is committing the act of deception is even worthy of being his son. When questioned, "How is it that you have found (the game) so quickly my son?",[261] Jacob uses the Lord's name in vain by giving God credit for his dishonest deeds, "Because the Lord your God granted me success."[262] Not only does Jacob blame the Lord for his own wickedness, but in doing so he does not even claim the Lord as his own, as he testified by saying "The Lord *your* God."

In the end, Jacob capitalized on the helplessness of his father and obtained the blessing:

> May God give you of the dew of heaven, and of the fatness of the earth, and plenty of grain and wine. Let peoples serve you, and nations bow down to you. Be lord over your brothers, and may your mother's sons bow down to you. Cursed be everyone who curses you, and blessed be everyone who blesses you![263]

The stealing of the blessing marked a pivotal moment in the life of Jacob. Though he had received the birthright by just means

---

[260]   Genesis 27:19
[261]   Genesis 27:20
[262]   Genesis 27:21
[263]   Genesis 27:27-29

which entitled him to receive the blessing of his fathers, he later "came in guile,"[264] obtaining the blessing through outright betrayal.

From this point on Jacob encountered humiliation upon humiliation. Yet, these humiliations, as we will see, were necessary for him to receive the gift of humility, to reconcile with Esau, to reconcile with God, and thus prepared him to build the domestic sanctuary. Jacob, by means of his selfish disposition, had developed the nearly automatic habit of grasping for greatness and using whatever was in his means to obtain what he thought should be his own. By means of humiliations God called Jacob to reconcile with his past and with his God. As we will see, Jacob repeatedly rejected the invitation to humility, causing harm to himself and those who would eventually become a part of his life.

---

[264]   See Genesis 27:35

# DAY 56

## JOSEPH'S DESIRE FOR GREATNESS

"Joseph, being a just man and unwilling to expose her (Mary) to shame, resolved to send her away quietly. But as he considered this, behold, an angel of the Lord appeared to him in a dream, saying, 'Joseph, son of David...'"[265] My dear brother, much has been said and will be said with regards to this concise passage from the Sacred Scriptures, which contains treasures worth meditating upon at length. For the purpose of this discussion we will study this text in light of Joseph's desire for greatness.

Though the angelic salutation may have surprised Joseph, the words the angel spoke, "Joseph, son of David," did not catch him off guard. Like most Jews of his time, Joseph was intimately aware of his lineage; a lineage flowing with the royal blood of Abraham, Isaac, Jacob and David. An underground king, but a king no less, Joseph, like his faithful comrades, eagerly desired the advent of the prophesied Messiah, a Messiah whose father Joseph might potentially be. This potential must have been a consideration at times, if not often, in the mind of Joseph, who being a son of David by nature also longed to be a son of David by grace.

Joseph desired to see the fulfillment of the promise given to Abraham, "descendents more numerous than the stars,"[266] and perhaps hoped to become, like his fathers, "a father of many nations."[267]

---

[265] Matthew 1:1:19-20
[266] Genesis 15:5
[267] Genesis 17:4

The thought of being a father to the Messiah may have inspired Joseph with a holy longing and a holy fear. The consideration of being called to such an incredible vocation must have created a tension in Joseph's soul between his recognition of a God-given vocation and the temptation for self-glorification. This tension became the very tool by which God prepared and purified Joseph for his holy vocation as father of the Son of God, and husband of the spouse of God.

When he betrothed Mary, Joseph's potential to become the father of the Messiah increased. Yet when the Virgin's pregnancy was revealed, any hope for such a glorious mission appeared to be all but dashed. Peering more deeply into the matter, we discover that Joseph's potential to be the father of the Messiah by means of his marriage to Mary must be questioned. For the angel of the Lord greeted Mary with the message "Behold thou shalt conceive in thy womb, and shalt bring forth a son; and thou shalt call his name Jesus."[268] But Mary responded, "How shall this be done, because I know not man?"[269] What can Mary's response mean? And how does her response relate to her relationship with Joseph?

Since Mary was betrothed to Joseph and soon to dwell with him as his wife, her question "how shall this be done, because I know not man" would seem unnecessary. For Mary would have surmised that after living with Joseph, the two of them would have had conjugal relations and the child of the Most High would have been the fruit of this sexual union. Indeed, the angel spoke to Mary in the future tense, "thou *shalt* conceive," which Mary would have understood as meaning that this would happen by means of her marital union with Joseph.

Mary's words to the angel indicate that she had made a prior decision, a decision to remain celibate. Mary did not fear the angel

---

[268]  Luke 1:31
[269]  Luke 1:34

but rather the angel's words. Mary was perplexed because she could not understand how she—being exclusively God's through a vow of virginity and not knowing man, that is, not being integrated with man's fallen ways— could conceive a child. Mary truly did not know the ways of man and therefore did not comprehend how the divine conception would occur.

Within this context we discover St. Joseph's humble character. Joseph, being aware of Mary's exclusive dedication to God, and in order to wed himself to Mary, sacrificed his hope for having children, precisely sacrificing any hope to father the Messiah, and therefore, shunned any selfish desire for greatness. Yet, God tested Joseph even further: after discovering the Virgin had conceived a child, Joseph could not help but to become fearful of the mystery within Mary, and therefore was forced to make a decision as to whether he would also sacrifice marriage, his relationship with Mary, and any hopes of being connected to this mystery.

My brother, what then can we say of Joseph and his desire for greatness in regards to Mary's pregnancy? Joseph renounced his desire for greatness in one of two ways, if not both. First, by means of dedicating himself to Mary by means of a celibate marriage Joseph set aside the desire to be the father of the Messiah. Second, by divorcing Mary quietly, Joseph makes the decision to detach himself definitively from all that seemed great. Regardless of whether or not Joseph had vowed himself to a celibate marriage, he did choose to renounce self-exaltation for the sake of fulfilling God's will.

Joseph, unlike Adam, did not attempt to be as God, nor did he deem his betrothed, as something to be grasped, but rather, emptied himself of all false desires for personal greatness, and therefore God exalted him as the model of all husbands and fathers.

Brother, within Joseph, God certainly planted the authentic and sincere desire for greatness. Yet how can we be certain as to whether or not Joseph's desire for greatness retained the true character of a disinterested desire to glorify God? Was Joseph's desire for greatness mingled with the false desire for self-exaltation?

By examining Joseph's response to the discovery of the pregnant Virgin Mary we will discover whether or not the son of David's desire for greatness was truly a desire to glorify the Great One, or simply a desire for the Great One to make him great.

# DAY 57

JOSEPH'S DESIRE FOR GREATNESS II

"Joseph, being a just man,"[270] "mediated upon the law both day and night,"[271] for so the psalmist tells us that the just man does. This interior prayer life gave Joseph's exterior actions form: the form of justness. With consistent forbearance, Joseph pressed into the scriptures, allowing the Word to be impressed upon his heart, and thus his actions were animated by divine life, enabling him to press the image of God, through his humble actions, upon the world surrounding him.

Obedience to, and fulfillment of, the law were the determining factors as to whether or not a Jew was regarded as just. Yet, fulfillment of the law without love is legalism, which Jesus so zealously condemned with his seven woes to the hypocrites,[272] emphasizing that the weightier matters of the law are "justice and mercy and faith."[273]

Justice, mercy, and faith can be likened to a stone foundation of the spiritual home which will not be shaken or crumble when the waves and torrents of sufferings and temptations come. And they will come. Justice, mercy, and faith are like a row of stones, each set upon the other, which solidify the foundation upon which the spiritual temple of God is built. Only a house with this three-tier

---

[270] Matthew 1:19

[271] See Psalm 1:2

[272] See Matthew 23

[273] Matthew 23: 23

foundation will be capable of supporting the great spiritual weight of the indwelling Triune God.

Each of these virtues constitutes a different level of spirituality that builds toward personal holiness. Justice can be described as keeping the law, or maintaining a holy fear of God. The virtue of mercy is linked to the love of neighbor, or having the gift of counsel. The theological virtue of faith represents the top level of this spiritual foundation, which can be described as a wholehearted belief and trust in God, and abandonment to His ways. In other words, true faith grants purity of heart, wisdom, and the ability to receive persecutions without doubting God's love.

Fear of the Lord, which is the beginning of Wisdom, inspires a man to fulfill the law, but primarily for reasons of self-preservation. A man initially follows the law to avoid the punishment that the law-giver inflicts if disobeyed. Though outwardly his ways have the character of being just, there may be no actual occurrence of interior transformation.

Mercy toward a neighbor acknowledges the demands of the law, yet moves beyond legalism in an effort to forgive the punishment due to the transgression committed. Such an act begins an interior transformation in the one who forgives. Thus the merciful fulfill the law with love by loving their neighbor.

Even this tremendous act of forgiveness can, at times, fall short by becoming alloyed with the impure motive of loving the creature as an end over and above the Creator, Who is man's true end.

Indeed, love of neighbor is never enough to make one perfect or perfect his relationship with God. Too often man loves the creature at the expense of loving the Creator above all things. Often a man forgives his brother, applying mercy only to sustain a relationship for selfish motives, afraid that the loss of the friendship would become a loss far too great to endure.

By exercising faith, however, a man subjects the law and love of neighbor to the Lord; placing each of these, in a detached manner, at His feet; waiting for God to direct him as to how he should respond in a particular situation. Faith becomes the row of stones at the top of the foundation that holds the fulfillment of the law and love of neighbor in place. This virtue of faith binds the foundation of the spiritual temple to the rest of the temple of God, that is, the person who hopes for residency in the permanent temple of God Himself.

Without the theological virtue of faith, justice and mercy are void of the power to save a man. Without faith the spiritual temple cannot be built. Faith draws down the animating power of the Holy Spirit which breathes life into our obedience to the law and our love of neighbor, perfecting all of our actions, granting us the hope of eternally dwelling in and with God.

Joseph, being a "just man," was disposed to fulfilling the law, yet understood fully that the just demands of the law upon a woman found pregnant prior to the consummation of a marriage was death. Without rejecting the law, but moved by love, Joseph applied his personal right, afforded by the Law, to be merciful to Mary, "resolving to send her away quietly."[274] Joseph fulfilled the law by acknowledging its just demands, while also being merciful to Mary, thus fulfilling the demands of the law with mercy. Most importantly, however, after Joseph had resolved to carry out this plan of obedience and mercy, he subjected both the law and his love for neighbor to the Lord.

"But as he considered this, an angel appeared to him in a dream."[275] My brother, see how Joseph presented his situation to the Lord, and though he was worn from the dilemma, he did not terminate his prayer but rather pressed on, even while he slept. Joseph's prayer was so intense that he was able to continue in prayer as he rested. The prayer life of Joseph echoes the Psalmist's words,

---

[274]   Matthew 1:19
[275]   Matthew 1:20

"I will bless the Lord Who gives me counsel; in the night also my heart instructs me."[276] In prayer Joseph is granted the answer to his conflicted desire for greatness, "Joseph, do not fear to take Mary your wife, for that which is conceived in her is of the Holy Spirit; she will bear a son, and you shall call His name Jesus, for He will save His people from their sins."[277]

By submitting the situation to God, Joseph proved that his longing for greatness was animated by his desire to glorify God. Joseph glorified God and God glorified the humble Joseph. Where Jacob took matters into his own hands, Joseph lifted his hands to God. Jacob grasped for the blessing of having nations bow down to him, while Joseph bowed down to the Lord and the Lord exalted Joseph as king of the King of the Jews. Where Jacob grasped and stole what was legally his, Joseph used his legal rights to release the Virgin, and in releasing her, he received not only God's Mother but also God's Son.

The example of Jacob teaches us never to become so attached to our own personal longings for greatness that we use our legal rights to take measures into our own hands, rather than lifting our hands to God in prayer and allowing Him to exalt us in due time. The example of Joseph should inspire us never to become so attached to the requirements of the law, or to loving our neighbor, that we neglect to give God pride of place. Friend, let us learn from Joseph the priority of submitting all matters to the Lord in prayer, requesting His guidance, for if we pray in this manner the Lord will certainly respond.

Though submitting the law and love of neighbor to the Lord is the proper response in all matters, doing so will make us vulnerable to humiliations of many kinds. Let us continue examining Jacob and Joseph and their encounters with humiliations.

---

[276]   Psalm 16:7
[277]   Matthew 1:20-21

# DAY 58

### HUMILIATIONS, THE PASSAGEWAY TO HUMILITY

Humiliations are the painful passageways to humility. We may either flee from these paths that are covered with thorns and thistles, or we may press into the thicket, discovering the way from self-enslavement to liberation from self. Those of interior strength will press on upon the path of humiliation, receiving the crown of humility.

Indeed, those who are of true interior strength will embrace humiliations, while others may view such persons as apparently weak. Those who resist and avoid humiliations may appear sleek and strong, but are actually interiorly weak, fainthearted, and prideful men, unable to subject themselves to the process of sanctification. Notice that Jacob's confession to his mother, "behold I am a smooth man,"[278] speaks not only of his physical body but also speaks of the spiritual reality of his sleekness, or his unwillingness to surrender to humiliations.

If we stay the course, my bother, the fire of humiliation will purify us, availing us the opportunity to reconcile ourselves with God, with our brothers, and even with ourselves. Each humiliation is an invitation to reconcile ourselves and all of our human relationships with God. By embracing humiliation rather than resorting to manipulation, a man will rise in peace as a new man in Christ. The fact that we have reconciled with man, not out of selfish motives,

---

[278] Genesis 27:11

but out of humility, is proof indeed that we have reconciled with God.

The prayer of perseverance is marked by many failings that actually light the path to great achievements. These failings are nothing less than humiliations that sting man's interior being, batter his ego, intimidate him, and tempt him to consider fleeing the vocational path that he has embarked upon.

Such humiliations are often the result of being misunderstood by another, misunderstanding another, being rejected by another, making an error, having a fault exposed, or committing a sin. These humiliations are almost never general, but specific to the interior person, piercing man's disordered ego with pin-point accuracy, penetrating his self-styled image with the reality that he is not God, but rather, a fallen creature utterly incapable of fulfilling the vocation of erecting the domestic sanctuary without the aid of the eternal Craftsman. Indeed, "if the Lord does not build the house in vain do its laborers labor."[279] Ironically, a multitude of humiliations will occur precisely within the context of building the domestic church, within the covenant of marriage, and in our relationships with our children. Rather than the domestic church being a place of refuge from humiliations, the domestic church *is* the place of purification and personal sanctity by means of humiliations.

Each humiliation may be considered as an epiphany, an awakening from the stupor of egoism, enlightening man's intellect with the refreshing reality of who he truly is: a creature completely dependent upon his Creator.

Though external humiliations are often most humiliating, each humiliation penetrates man's interior being regardless of its exterior manifestation. Dear brother, our awareness of our limitedness is not dependent upon others' awareness of our limitedness; for we ourselves are keenly aware of how limited we are, though we

---

[279]  Psalm 127

often avoid admitting this truth. More often than not, others will not perceive our personal limitedness, yet we perceive it intimately. Even if your limitedness lies hidden from your brother it is real nonetheless.

A man who does not admit his own limitedness displays himself as being without weakness or limitation, thus demonstrating how limited is his ability to acknowledge his own weakness. Such a man will often convince himself that he has no personal weakness and thereby proves that he is limited and clouded in his self-awareness. This makes the limitedness that he hides most evident to all.

Humiliations that occur within family life are painfully acute, but are no less gifts from God. They are a grace loaded with the purifying fire of the Holy Spirit that invite one to embrace the virtue of humility, which is an essential characteristic of a father's interior strength. Yes, dear brother, to become strong we must admit our weaknesses and to become great fathers we must humble ourselves before the greatest Father. Indeed, "the Lord raises those who are bowed down"[280] and "opposes the proud but lifts up the lowly."[281]

There have existed those faithful few who have had no need of humiliations to advance in the virtue of humility. Although humiliations are not necessary for all persons to increase in humility, humility is necessary for all to embrace humiliations. For most, humiliations are a pivotal opportunity to receive and advance in the exalted virtue of humility.

As we encounter a personal humiliation we will be tempted to react with our passions, emotionally defending our ego, attempting to deny our own personal deficiency. During this collision of our pride and humiliation we must sift through our passions, straining out all that is emotional, while retaining only prudence's honest

---

[280] Psalm 146
[281] See Luke 1:52

assessment of ourselves and the situation. In other words, after being humiliated, regardless of whether or not others are aware of it, we must resist the temptation to indulge our pride by defending our ego. O how difficult this is! By embracing this blow to our pride we will be granted the opportunity to choose the exalted virtue of humility.

If we desire to grow in strength, we must develop humility, and if we are to develop humility, we must allow our ego to become vulnerable, permitting the humiliation to crush our pride. We will grow in humility as we suppress our ego, and in suppressing our ego we will grow further in humility; and growing further in humility we will more readily admit our own limitedness. By admitting our own limitedness we will allow the unlimited, redemptive grace of God to strengthen us, exalting our own fatherhood, and bringing glory to the Fatherhood of God.

# DAY 59

## JACOB'S HUMILIATION

Predestined though Jacob was to supplant Esau, the guile with which he supplanted his elder brother became the source of many humiliations, trials, and setbacks, which not only affected Jacob personally, but also rippled out to those who became close to him.

Jacob's act of guile caused him to become the object of Esau's hatred.

> Now Esau hated Jacob because of the blessing with which his father had blessed him, and Esau said to himself, "The days of mourning my father are approaching; then I will kill my brother Jacob." But the words of Esau her older son were told to Rebekah; so she sent and called Jacob her younger son, and said to him, "Behold, your brother Esau comforts himself by planning to kill you. Now therefore, my son, obey my voice; arise, flee to Laban my brother in Haran, and stay with him a while, until your brother's fury turns away; until your brother's anger turns away, and he forgets what you have done to him; then I will send, and fetch you from there. Why should I be bereft of you both in one day?"[282]

Jacob, confronted by the fact that his life was in danger, was forced into exile. In other words Jacob was humiliated. Jacob was unable to contend with the strength and hatred of Esau, and so, in cowardice, he fled to a distant land. Just as Rebekah had disguised

---

[282]    Genesis 27:41 -45

Jacob with the skins of kids to help him obtain the blessing of his fathers, so did she also cover Jacob's humiliation by convincing her dying husband Isaac that Jacob could not remain in Canaan and marry one of the Hittite women, lest her life and his be in danger.

Isaac, convinced by Rebekah's plea,

> called Jacob and blessed him, and charged him, "You shall not marry one of the Canaanite women. Arise, go to Paddan-aram to the house of Bethuel your mother's father; and take as your wife from there one of the daughters of Laban your mother's brother." Then Isaac proceeded with the final blessing, "God Almighty bless you and make you fruitful and multiply you, that you may become a company of peoples. May he give the blessing of Abraham to you and to your descendents with you, that you may take possession of the land of your sojournings which God gave to Abraham!" Thus Isaac sent Jacob away.[283]

The first of Jacob's humiliations came from his father Isaac, who, convinced by Rebekah, "sent Jacob away...to Laban, the brother of Rebekah,"[284] to marry one of his daughters. Yet the underlying reason for sending Jacob away was Rebekah's fear that the resentful Esau would carry out his vengeful plot to murder him, and perhaps even her. Upon receiving the blessing of Isaac, Jacob was forced to leave his native place of birth, his father and mother, his very home, and become an exile in a foreign land.

My brother, how important it is that we meditate upon this lesson: Though Jacob was chosen and blessed by God to become the father of many "descendants like the dust of the earth,"[285] he was also sent into exile because of his guile. Blessed by his father to

---

[283]  Genesis 28:1-3
[284]  Genesis 28:5
[285]  Genesis 28:14

receive the land, Jacob became a wanderer without a home; blessed to rule over his brother, he became a fugitive fleeing from his new subject; blessed to be a blessing he became, as we will see, one who brought upon others the sufferings of his past.

Learn, my brother, from the bitter life of Jacob that duplicity is not acceptable in the sight of the simple and pure God, but is an abomination from which we must repent. Just as the Lord drove Jacob into exile, so he will do to each of us in order to bring about within us repentance and reconciliation with our past.

Jacob's exile became an intense period of purification wherein God formed and instructed his heart, leading him to repent of his own self-reliance and become dependent upon the ways of the Lord. We may either choose to send our self-reliance into exile by confronting our past, or we will receive from God the just measure of exile as a time to reflect and discover the true path home.

Obeying his father's command, Jacob left his childhood home, fleeing to the house of Laban, his mother's brother. While on his journey he

came to a certain place, and stayed there that night, because the sun had set. Taking one of the stones of the place, he put it under his head and lay down in that place to sleep. And he dreamed that there was a ladder set up on the earth, and the top of it reached to heaven; and behold, the angels of God were ascending and descending on it! And behold, the LORD stood above it and said, "I am the LORD, the God of Abraham your father and the God of Isaac; the land on which you lie I will give to you and to your descendants; and your descendants shall be like the dust of the earth, and you shall spread abroad to the west and to the east and to the north and to the south; and by you and your descendants shall all the families of the earth bless themselves. Behold, I am with you and will keep you wherever you go, and will bring you back to this land; for I will not leave you until I have done that of which I have spoken to you." Then Jacob awoke from his sleep and said, "Surely the LORD is in this place; and I did not know it." And he was afraid, and said, "How awesome is this place! This is none other than the house of God, and this is the gate of heaven."

At first glance it appears that this dream wherein the Lord spoke to Jacob will prove to be a decisive turning point in his life. The Lord promised His presence, His blessing, the land, and descendants more numerous than the dust of the earth. In other words, the Lord proves Himself to be a Father, a pure Gift to Jacob. The Lord pledged to Jacob these tremendous blessings not because of any works Jacob had done, but simply because God desired to do so. In response, Jacob "set up a pillar and poured oil on the top of it. and called the name of that place Bethel,"[286] that is, the house of God.

Jacobs' response, however, demonstrates that he did not understand the generous nature of God, for he was still "afraid" and made a vow saying,

If God will be with me, and will keep me in this way that I go, and will give me bread to eat and clothing to wear, so that I come again to my father's house in peace, then the Lord shall be my God, and this stone, which I have set up for a pillar, shall be God's house; and of all that thou givest me I will give the tenth to thee.[287]

Jacob's words demonstrate that he was still attempting to secure God's generosity by human means: "If God does this, then I will do that." "If God does this for me, then the Lord shall be my God."

At first glance it appears that Jacob is saying to *himself,* "If God gives me what I want, then I will allow him to be my God."

---

[286]   Genesis 28:18-19

[287]   Genesis 28:20 - 22

However, we come to understand that Jacob is actually talking *to* the Lord, for at the end of the prayer he says, "And of all that thou givest me I will give the tenth to thee."[288] This indicates that Jacob knows within his heart that God is listening. By addressing God as Thou at the end of his statement, Jacob reveals that he said these things to ensure the Lord would overhear. In other words, Jacob refused to receive the complete, self-giving generosity of God, but rather attempted to manipulate God and work out a deal, hoping to benefit himself.

Though Jacob received the Lord's promise, he had not surrendered his past methods of manipulation and grasping, nor had he allowed God to transform him into a son who receives the generous love of the Father. God gave Jacob Himself, but Jacob did not surrender himself to God. Holding on to and hiding his past, Jacob inevitably passed on the pain of his guile to those he would eventually encounter.

[288]   Genesis 28:20-22

# DAY 60

## JACOB'S HUMILIATION II

Jacob continued on his journey until he came to

> a well in a field where three flocks of sheep were lying beside it, for out of that well the flocks were watered. The stone of the well's mouth was large, and when all the flocks were gathered there, the shepherds would roll the stone from the mouth of the well, and water the sheep, and put the stone back in its place upon the mouth of the well.[289]

Now Jacob approached the shepherds who revealed that they were from Haran where Laban, his mother's brother lived, and that Rachel, Laban's daughter, was coming with the sheep. Jacob, still attempting to control the situation, wanted the shepherds to depart so that he could be alone with Rachel, for he said,

> "It is not time for the animals to be gathered together; water the sheep and go, pasture them." But they said, "We cannot until all the flocks are gathered together, and the stone is rolled from the mouth of the well, then we water the sheep."[290]

While he was still speaking with them, Rachel came with her father's sheep; for she kept them. Now when Jacob saw Rachel

---

[289]   Genesis 29:2-4
[290]   Genesis 28:7-8

the daughter of Laban his mother's brother, Jacob went up and
rolled the stone from the well's mouth, and watered the flock of
Laban his mother's brother.[291]

In other words, Jacob uses the situation to his advantage by
demonstrating his strength to impress Rachel, who was "beautiful
and lovely,"[292] by rolling the rock aside to water her flocks.

Later, after Jacob had lived in the home of Laban for one
month, Laban asked Jacob,

"what shall your wages be?" Now Laban had two daughters; the
name of the older was Leah, and the name of the younger was
Rachel. Leah's eyes were weak, but Rachel was beautiful and
lovely. Jacob loved Rachel; and he said, "I will serve you seven years
for your younger daughter Rachel." Laban said, "It is better that I
give her to you than that I should give her to any other man; stay
with me."

Jacob's words offer great insight into the disposition of his soul.
They express an interior belief that the greater the gift, the more
one should strive to *earn* the gift. Again, this proposal to Laban is
much like the *deal* Jacob made with God, demonstrating that Jacob
still has a disposition of grasping rather than one of receptivity to
God.

Notice that Laban did not definitively grant the request of
Jacob, but stated that it was better if Rachel were to be with Jacob
than another man. The reason for this evasiveness was that in
Laban's culture it was customary for a father to marry off his eldest
daughter first, before giving the younger in marriage. Laban's words
reveal that he was skilled in the art of manipulation; manipulation

---

[291]   Genesis 28: 9-10

[292]   Genesis 29:17

like that which Jacob was accustomed to using to obtain what he desired.

Indeed, Jacob loved Rachel enough to serve Laban for seven years of service in exchange for her, and the seven years "seemed to him but a few days because of the love he had for her."[293] In his encounter with Rachel, Jacob perceived an opportunity to flee from his troubled past, envisioning a better future with a woman whom he had hoped to be the solution to his problems. Many men foolishly look to woman, believing that her love will become for them a solution to the emptiness, misery and loneliness of their past. No woman, however, can provide a man this type of fulfillment. Often, a man sees a woman as an escape from his damaged self, only to damage the woman by imprisoning her in his past.

If a man who is unhappy clings to a woman, he draws her into his unhappiness. If a man has not submitted to God his hidden past, he cannot help but expose her to the pain of his shame. It is a lie to believe that the life we bring to the sacrament of marriage is a completely new life, separated from the life we have lived. Our thoughts, actions, dispositions, beliefs, and experiences are the manifestation of many years of growth and maturation which have been ingrained into our being and are naturally a part of the person that we bring to the marriage. The self a man gives to his wife must be transformed by our Lord, lest he bring to the marriage the scandal, disorders, and wounds of his past, thus wounding the bride he has come to love. This is precisely what Jacob did to the family of Laban.

After fulfilling the agreement he had made with Laban, Jacob, after seven years, was ready to take Rachel as his wife.

> Then Jacob said to Laban, "Give me my wife that I may go in to
> her, for my time is completed." So Laban gathered together all the

---

[293]  Genesis 29:20

men of the place, and made a feast. But in the evening he took his
daughter Leah and brought her to Jacob; and he went into her.
And in the morning, behold, it was Leah; and Jacob said to Laban,
"What is this you have done to me?" Laban said, "It is not so done
in our country, to give the younger before the first-born. Complete
the week of this one, and we will give the other also in return for
serving me another seven years."[294]

Jacob had been beguiled by Laban, reaping what he had sown
by deceiving his father Isaac. Instead of receiving Rachel in marriage, Jacob awoke realizing that he had consummated a marriage
with Leah the elder daughter of Laban. In the darkness of his
father's blindness, after feasting with Isaac, Jacob duped his father
into granting him the blessing of the fathers. In the darkness of the
night and during the wedding feast, Laban duped Jacob, replacing
the woman he desired with a woman he did not want. Shedding its
light, morning brought mourning into the confused heart of Jacob.

In the process of fleeing to woman for a new hope and solace,
Jacob brought the disgrace of his past, so full of guile, deceit, con-
tention, and un-reconciled relationships, to Leah and eventually
Rachel. Jacob not only multiplied his wives but also his troubles.
Jacob not only suffered the humiliation of exile, but he also doubled
his humiliation by "exposing woman to shame,"[295] that is, by bring-
ing the shame of his deceitful, damaged past into the present life of
Leah and Rachel, affecting them in a most troubling way.

My brother, as we read the account of Jacob's humiliation, we
cannot help but to have pity on Jacob while also resenting the wickedness of Laban. Yet it was this same wickedness that enabled Jacob
to obtain the blessing from his father. Understand, dear brother,
that God allowed these humiliations to occur in Jacob's life to serve

---

[294] Genesis 29:21-30
[295] Matthew 1:19

as an invitation for Jacob to reconcile his past to God. Indeed, Jacob had not repented of his guile, and therefore was subjected to guile in order to move him toward repentance.

Returning to the first encounter between Jacob and Rachel, when Jacob so impressively rolled back the stone of Laban's well as proof of his exterior strength and manhood, we arrive at a deeper understanding of the rock and the well. Jacob rolled back the stone of the well to impress Rachel with his exterior strength, yet he was not moved enough by the rock at Bethel to have the interior strength to reconcile with his past before involving a woman in his life.

The rock at Bethel was the sign of the presence of the Living God Who provides the living waters from which all men should drink. Jacob teaches us that the interior strength provided by the Rock from Whom the living waters flow is of greater necessity than any show of exterior masculinity. Indeed, the interior strength of a man gives his exterior life form, not vice versa.

If a man desires to build the domestic church, he must pursue holiness with his entire being; for a man cannot give what he does not have. If his interior person is lacking, his exterior expression of self will be lacking. Therefore let us, my brother, reconcile ourselves to God, receive His healing, and refuse to expose our wives to the shame of our deceitful, lustful pasts.

# DAY 61

The good-willed action of vowing himself to Mary allowed Joseph to become susceptible to many humiliations. The fact that Joseph took the reality of Mary's pregnancy to prayer, even into his sleep, indicates that the seriousness of Mary's pregnancy caused Joseph great concern, if not anxiety. Regardless of how he might respond, Joseph could not avoid being cut to the heart by incisive humiliations; his wife, who vowed herself to him in fidelity, was pregnant without his cooperation.

Let us briefly consider the content of Joseph's humiliations: First, the wife that he was betrothed to was discovered pregnant without his cooperation. Second, Joseph's character came under question in regards to the suspicion that he was the cause of Mary's pregnancy. Third, Joseph was helpless in that there was no immediate solution to his dilemma. If Joseph had remained with Mary he would have appeared to be unchaste, and if he departed from her he would have appeared to agree with the suspicions of the villagers that Mary had been faithless. But most of all, Joseph's greatest humiliation was the loss of Mary, and perhaps, at some level, the question of whether or not his actions would be misunderstood by Mary.

It is within the context of this intense trial that we discover the altruistic character of St. Joseph. Before unveiling the noble and virtuous quality of this just man, let us briefly return to Jacob and understand the digressive steps that initially led him away from true greatness.

First, Jacob ran to woman, believing that Rachel was the answer to his longing for fulfillment. Second, he believed that he could *earn* her by means of years of labor and that he could become *worthy* of her. Third, by clinging to Rachel without repenting of his past, he exposed her to shame, bringing curse after curse upon her.

Let us now turn to Joseph and compare his steps of progression, which led him to answer his call to greatness, with the pattern of Jacob. First, though Joseph loved Mary with a husband's love, he nevertheless understood clearly that Mary was not the answer to his longing for fulfillment, as proven by his willingness to "divorce her quietly." Second, though Mary's pregnancy appeared to the world to be of scandalous nature, Joseph was inclined to believe that divine intervention had indeed occurred. Rather than jockeying for a position of self-glory by positioning himself as Mary's savior, Joseph believed himself unworthy of Mary and unable to earn the position of husband of the Mother of God. Third, Joseph fled from Mary, refusing to expose her to the shame of men; he refused to unveil her mystery. "Joseph being a just man, and unwilling to expose her (Mary) to shame, resolved to send her away quietly."[296] Indeed,

> the verb "deigmatizo" translated here as "expose her to shame" and "apoluo" translated here as "divorce," [can be validly translated, as] proposed by the Jesuit scripture scholar Fr. Ignace de la Potterie, "But Joseph, her spouse, who was a just man, and who did not wish to unveil (her mystery), resolved to secretly separate (himself) from her." From this we get a better understanding of the insight of St. Bernard of Clairvaux who wrote, "Why did he wish to leave her?... He saw, with sacred astonishment, that she bore a special quality of the divine presence, and while not being able to understand this mystery, he wished to leave her." (Hom. "Super Missus

---

[296]  Matthew 1:19

Est") St. Thomas Aquinas reiterates this insight in his Summa Theologica writing, "Joseph wanted to give the Virgin her liberty, not because he suspected her of adultery, but out of respect for her sanctity he feared to live together with her." (Supplementum III, q.62, art. 3) St. Joseph recognized the virtue necessary to protect such a profound mystery. He feared that in human weakness, he might defile the mystery by remaining close. Like St. Peter and the centurion who both said, "I am not worthy," St. Joseph did not consider himself virtuous enough to veil this mystery by his presence; rather he thought he could do so better by his absence.[297]

My brother, see how Joseph chose not to subject woman to the limits and dullness of man's mind, but spared her the shame that can so often be caused by man's impulsive emotional responses. Unlike Jacob, who fled from humiliation, hoping to receive solace and consolation in woman, and instead heaped the wounds of his past upon her, exposing her to shame, Joseph refused to subject the Virgin, so full of grace, to the miserable ways of men.

Joseph could have erred in two ways: first he could have pretended that the child was his own, grasping at some solution to avoid becoming a public spectacle, thus dismissing the true significance of Mary's pregnancy and falsely pretending that the situation was not of grave importance. Or Joseph could have renounced the child and Mary altogether, thus clearing his name. Joseph rather executed the most painful action: He did not condemn Mary or attempt to hide or suppress the dilemma. He did not manipulate the situation to make himself appear justified, but rather trusted God and embraced the humiliation, thus embracing humility. Unlike Jacob, who grasped at the objects of his desire and was thus exposed, Joseph embraced God's will and was justified. The

---

[297]   Father Boniface Hicks, O.S.B., *Blessed Be St. Joseph Her Most Chaste Spouse*, Theology of the Body Institute 2012, http://s450454794.online-home.us/blessed-be-st-joseph-her-most-chaste-spouse/

humiliated Joseph did not resist the humiliation but embraced it, receiving with it the blessings that accompany the grand virtue of humility.

Fleeing from woman, Joseph expressed his desire to protect her from the corruption of fallen man and man's long history of sin, a disorder that began with Adam who was unwilling to protect the virgin Eve from shame. In addition to Joseph's unwillingness to expose the Virgin to the fallen nature of man, he was also unwilling to burden her with the pressure of being the source of his consolation and fulfillment. "It is better to trust in God than in princes,"[298] and princesses for that matter. Joseph's resolution to send Mary away quietly, rather than clinging to her or having her legally executed, demonstrated his authentic detachment from the woman he loved and his attachment to the God Who created her. By dismissing the Virgin, Joseph was not dismissing himself from the situation, nor was he taking control of the situation; he was placing it in God's hands. This is true humility.

---

[298]   Psalm 118

# DAY 62

SEEKING GREATNESS WITH HUMILITY

The dream of Jacob and the dream of Joseph proved to be pivotal events in each of their lives. Each man's dreams provided him with ample means to reconcile himself to God before pressing forward and entering into the covenant of marriage. Jacob awoke from his dream and failed to reconcile his selfish past with God, and thus retained his distorted view of a God who bargains and trades with man. This lack of reconciliation with God brought spiritual disease and division into his marriages.

Joseph, however, awoke from his dream, reconciled with God, and became a gift to his betrothed, and was thus able to transfer the redemptive grace he received to his bride and Son to be.

Indeed, we should love our bride by shielding her from the shame of our sin. It is our duty as husbands, dear brother, to become guardians of the garden of woman, protecting her, doing all in our power to never expose her to shame. Every man, to some degree, is bound by lust and pride. Rather than hiding our past like Jacob, we must repent of our lustful and prideful dispositions and reconcile our past, so full of faults, sins, and errors, with God, with Whom "are mercy and forgiveness" and "the fullness of redemption."[299]

If we expose our shame to God, bearing our sinful heritage to His healing power, we will become reconciled with Him and begin to experience the power of Christ's redemption. Upon being reconciled with the Father we can begin to act as true fathers without

---

[299]  See Psalm 130

resorting to using, grasping, or lusting, and thus we will spare our wives from our sinful past, and become more readily equipped to begin the project of building the domestic church.

Dear brother, as you press on in your pursuit of building the domestic church, you will fail and encounter various humiliations; embrace them. These humiliations will prove to be the very crucible that will refine you into a man of humility who can face the demands of building the domestic church.

Brother, be not like those who flee from humiliations. By doing so they become cowards, resisting the process of purification that transforms one into a saint. "Do not be surprised at the fiery ordeal which comes upon you to prove you, as though something strange were happening to you,"[300] but embrace this purification, for the Holy Spirit that is leading you "is no cowardly spirit."[301] Become little, humble; drink from the waters of humiliation, and these life-giving waters will grant you humility.

Indeed, to become great, one must paradoxically become little, or rather reconcile himself with his littleness. Humility has been defined as total self-awareness. For example, Mary proclaims that she is the "handmaid of the Lord,"[302] but also states that her "soul magnifies the Lord."[303] Our Lord Himself stated that the Father was greater than He,[304] and yet also proclaimed that He and the Father are One,[305] and that when one sees Him he sees the Father.[306] Joseph, also, by secretly leaving Mary, believing himself unworthy of her, became the one whom God chose to be worthy of receiving her "into his own."

---

[300]   1 Peter 4:12

[301]   2 Timothy 1:7

[302]   Luke 1:38

[303]   Luke 1:46

[304]   See John 14:28

[305]   See John 10:30

[306]   See John 14:7

Humility is the acceptance of who we are, both the good and bad aspects. The humble man believes that God's plan consists of using men who are not perfect to transmit the riches of His love. Indeed, God "is able to do all things more abundantly than we desire or understand, according to the power that worketh in us."[307]

Humility is the reality of who we are and Who God is within us. "For when we are weak, then we are powerful."[308] Indeed, if we confess our littleness, we will allow God's greatness to take hold of our lives, animating our actions, enabling us to do far greater things than ever imagined.

Reconcile yourself to your littleness and you will begin to reconcile yourself with your very greatness. You can be assured of this: if you, as a fallen creature, reconcile yourself with your littleness, you will reconcile yourself with the redemption offered by Christ, which confers the very power to become like Christ. Yes, my brother, by becoming little, we make room within us for the Great One to dwell. Yet, if we do not provide space for the indwelling of God, but rather fill that space with our maligned ambitions for self-glorification, we will suffer from a condition of permanent smallness, void of meaning and value. Littleness, as a means to greatness, is indeed a great gain, whereas self-exaltedness that ends in smallness is a tragic loss.

Choose littleness; cherish her; embrace her, and you will discover her sweetness. For she appears lonely, but with her you will receive the comfort of true friendship; she appears unnoticed, but as her companion your true self will be revealed; although her well appears empty, yet drinking of her you will be full and your thirst quenched even as you continue to thirst for her all the more. Therefore, reconcile with your littleness so that the Word, Who became enrobed in the flesh of a babe, can transform you from a child into a king.

---

[307] Ephesians 3:20
[308] See 2 Corinthians 12:10

*Wrestling with God:*
*the Virtue of Fortitude*

# DAY 63

The act of rising humbly from a humiliation is always assisted, if not animated, by the virtue of fortitude, which enables a man to enter into the arena of the spiritual battle, wherein he fights with the tenacious demons that tempt one to resist the will of God. This act of fortitude is flesh upon the skeleton of humility; a substantial exterior expression of man's interior resolution to walk uncompromisingly with God, heedless of the shame brought about by humiliation. Such an expression is a self-determined act of the will, a fundamental decision from the depths of a man's being to defeat the inordinate passions within himself. To choose to arise from humiliations, and embrace humility, and act with fortitude cannot be reduced to a reaction fueled by emotions, but requires that a man masters his own passions.

Just as the Lord Jesus allowed Himself to be crushed beneath the incredible burden of the cross, and nevertheless rose each time, we too must rise from our failings, weaknesses, and errors, growing in humility amidst these humiliations, and press into the struggle known as "Wrestling with God."

Wrestling with God can be defined as the interior battle against oneself, one's sinful past, and one's inordinate desires, with the help and grace of God. In other words, a man does not wrestle against God, as though he could experience victory over the Almighty, but rather wrestles with God, as a partner; a comrade, against himself, to defeat what is chained by pride, setting the real man free.

Upon recognizing God's ways as different, if not counter to our own habits, we may feel as though God is suppressing our passions and desires; but the truth is that our disordered passions oppress us. Through prayer, discernment, and growth in Godly knowledge, we will discover that God does not oppress us, but rather aids our conscience with knowledge of Himself and the demands of love.

To wrestle with oneself is an act of the will, which strives to recognize God as God and man as man. By this act we submit ourselves to God, asking for His aid, not attempting pridefully to achieve the call to greatness by our own strength alone. Though it may sound ridiculous, many—even apparently faithful men—are too prideful to ask for God's help, especially in the matters that appear to be the most insignificant. The ego causes man to think, "I can do this myself, I don't need God's help," or "I do not want to bother God with this trivial matter, I will handle this myself." By choosing to act in such a manner, man has rejected the free gift of God's generous assistance, and even if such a man achieves the immediate proximate goal, he nevertheless fails to learn dependence upon the heavenly Father. Indeed, Our Lord Himself said, "apart from me you can do nothing,"[309] and elsewhere the apostle says that with God all things are possible.[310]

## Wrestling With God: The Three Components

Wrestling with God consists of three components: first, a father must overcome his personal resistance to God's will and ask for God's assistance in his pursuit to raise a holy family. Second, a man must reconcile his past with God, making peace with God and with himself to ensure that he transmits the peace of God to

---

[309]   John 15:5
[310]   See Philippians 4:13

his family. By doing so, a father will avoid bringing the cancer of his sins to the domestic church. By submitting your being and your past to God, and by following His promptings to reconcile with those you may have injured, you, my brother, will be given the third component of "Wrestling with God": the gift of fortitude.

# DAY 64

## ACCEPTANCE OF GOD'S WILL

### *Jacob's Acceptance of God's Will*

After serving his father-in-law for twenty years,

> Jacob saw that Laban did not regard him with favor as before.
> Then the LORD said to Jacob, "Return to the land of your fathers
> and to your kindred and I will be with you,"[311] and again, "I have
> seen all that Laban is doing to you. I am the God of Bethel, where
> you anointed a pillar and made a vow to me. Now arise, go forth
> from this land, and return to the land of your birth."[312]

To return to the land of his birth, the land of his fathers and the
land of his kindred, meant that Jacob would inevitably encounter
his brother, Esau. Facing this fact demanded an act of the will, a
fundamental decision to submit to the God Who promised to be
with Him and help him face his past, a past full of un-reconciled
relationships. We cannot underestimate Jacob's internal temptation
to resist the command of the Lord and attempt to carve out his own
future under his own direction and powers.

Issuing this command, the Lord was challenging Jacob to face
his past, to trust that the path of reconciliation was the path that
could afford him the foundation of peace upon which his life and

---

[311] Genesis 31: 3

[312] Genesis 31:14

family could be built. Remembering that the last desire of Esau was to murder the brother who stole "his" blessing, Jacob understood that by returning to the land of his fathers he was potentially endangering his life and the lives of his family. Fear re-entered Jacob's life, becoming an undeniable temptation in the process of accepting God's will. Questions such as "who is to be feared more, God or Esau?", or "Is there a way other than the ways of God that will provide an ample solution to the dilemma?", must have circulated in the anxious mind of Jacob.

Fear is the root of all temptations, for it strikes at trust, the very foundation of a relationship between God and man, like an ax at the base of a tree, threatening to destroy the previously developed life of the person. Indeed, as our Lord said, "Fear is useless, trust is what is needed."[313] Yet when fear shakes the calm of a man's soul, he can opt to make the uselessness of fear useful, understanding that the temptation is an alarm that prompts him to turn away from its lure toward doubt and mistrust of God, and rather embrace a renewed trust in his heavenly Father.

On this occasion, Jacob reacted differently than in the past, proving that his character had been transformed by his many humiliations. When Jacob heard the words, "I am the God of Bethel where you anointed the pillar and made a vow to me,"[314] he understood that God had more than kept His promise by providing for him and blessing him abundantly over the last twenty years. Now it was time for Jacob to fulfill his promise made previously to God: "If God will be with me, and will keep me in this way that I go, and will give me bread to eat and clothing to wear, so that I come again to my father's house in peace, then the Lord shall be my God."[315]

---

[313]   Luke 8:50
[314]   Genesis 31:13
[315]   Genesis 28:21

While Jacob desired the gifts of God, God desired Jacob, wanting him to accept Him as his God. God was not merely concerned with Jacob's temporal affairs, but used temporal blessings to enable Jacob to realize that God loved him as a father and desired reconciliation with him.

Setting his face toward the land of Edom, his homeland,

> Jacob sent messengers before him to Esau his brother in the land of Seir, the country of Edom, instructing them, "Thus you shall say to *my lord* Esau: Thus says *your servant* Jacob, 'I have sojourned with Laban, and stayed until now; and I have oxen, asses, flocks, menservants, and maidservants; and I have sent to tell *my lord* in order that I may find favor in your sight.'"[316]

Notice, my brother, the transformation which was occurring in Jacob. In a single statement Jacob thrice confesses himself the servant of Esau, referring to Esau as his Lord, thus demonstrating that he had embraced the virtue of humility.

> And the messengers returned to Jacob, saying, "We came to your brother Esau, and he is coming to meet you, and four hundred men with him." Then Jacob was greatly afraid and distressed; and he divided the people that were with him, and the flocks and herds and camels, into two companies, thinking, "If Esau comes to the one company and destroys it, then the company which is left will escape."[317]

It seems as though Jacob, once again, was depending upon his own methods of trickery, which appeared quite justifiable considering the foreboding fear. Like Joseph, however, Jacob was being

---

[316]   Genesis 32:3-5, emphasis added
[317]   Genesis 32:6-8

faithful to the law, to the command of God, to love his neighbor, and ultimately to the Lord, first by fulfilling the command to return to his father's land, and next by seeking reconciliation with his brother Esau. Like Joseph, Jacob took all of these matters to the Lord:

> O God of my father Abraham and God of my father Isaac, O Lord who didst say to me, "return to your country and to your kindred, and I will do you good"; I am not worthy of the least of all the steadfast love and all the faithfulness which thou hast shown to thy servant, for with only my staff I crossed this Jordan; and now I have become two companies. Deliver me, I pray thee, from the hand of my brother, from the hand of Esau, for I fear him, lest he come and slay us all, the mothers with the children. But thou didst say, "I will do you good, and make your descendants as the sand of the sea, which cannot be numbered for multitude."[318]

See, my brother, how Jacob became a new man, rising from his humiliations, refusing to use or beguile others, and thus surrendering in a humble act of fortitude to his God. Indeed, he admitted his humble state by confessing to God, "I am not worthy of the least of the steadfast love and all the faithfulness which thou has shown to thy servant," and regarding Esau he also said, "I fear him."

With these statements Jacob professed his identity as God's own servant, while also expressing his profound humility and dependence upon God. Yet Jacob also expressed that a fundamental transformation had occurred in his being by stating that his concern was not only for himself, as was his way previously, but was also for the mothers and the children: "for I fear him, lest he come and slay us all, the mothers with the children."

---

[318]   Genesis 32:9-32 emphasis added

My brother, Jacob faced humiliation upon humiliation and finally, after the constant invitation to reconcile himself to God, he arose from these humiliations, embracing humility, and by receiving the gift of humility finally became capable of receiving the virtue of holy fortitude.

# DAY 65

### JOSEPH'S ACCEPTANCE OF GOD'S WILL

At the heart and center of every moral decision is the decisive battle against the desire to "be as gods knowing good and evil."[319] In other words, a man must decide whether or not he should trust the God Who determines what is good and what is evil or rather entrust himself with the task of deciding for himself what is good and what is evil. By neglecting to accept what God has deemed good, and determining what is good for himself, man errs and strays from the God-given path that leads to greatness.

This dynamic is exemplified by humanity's first parents, who, although experiencing the vitality and joy of original goodness, fell prey to the temptation to choose their will over God's will.

> Now the serpent was more subtle than any of the beasts of the earth which the Lord God had made. And he said to the woman: Why hath God commanded you, that you should not eat of every tree of paradise? And the woman answered him, saying: Of the fruit of the trees that are in paradise we do eat: But of the fruit of the tree which is in the midst of paradise, God hath commanded us that we should not eat; and that we should not touch it, lest perhaps we die. And the serpent said to the woman: No, you shall not die the death. For God doth know that in what day soever you shall eat thereof, your eyes shall be opened: and you shall be as Gods, knowing good and evil. And the woman saw that the tree

---

[319] Genesis 3:5

was good to eat, and fair to the eyes, and delightful to behold: and
she took of the fruit thereof, and did eat, and gave to her husband,
who did eat. And the eyes of them both were opened: and when
they perceived themselves to be naked, they sewed together fig
leaves, and made themselves aprons.[320]

From this account we gain insight into the profound effects
caused by a man's decision to determine what he thinks is best
for himself, rather than what God knows to be best for him.
Adam, created and called by God to "dress and keep" the garden
of paradise,[321] neglected his duty and fell into the temptation that
Satan had set before him. The Hebrew words, "dress" (abad), and
"keep," (shamar) can be interpreted as "to serve" and "to guard and
protect", while the word garden, rich with biblical symbolism, can
signify woman and her interior person: "My sister, my spouse, is a
garden enclosed, a garden enclosed, a fountain sealed up."[322]

Adam's vocation, his call to greatness, can be explained in part
as his duty to defend and serve his wife, protecting her from having
her dignity stripped from her. It was Adam's duty to "dress" Eve,
that is, to veil the purity of her nakedness from the shame of evil.
Adam was called by God to "shamar" Eve from "shame."

Indeed, before the fall, Adam dressed Eve's nakedness with the
pure gaze of disinterested love, veiling her from the shame of lust.
However, Adam eventually denied his vocational duty to defend
his bride, and rather than "dressing her" with purity by defending her from the serpent, he allowed her to become subject to the
temptation of lust: "and the woman saw that the tree was good to
eat, and fair to the eyes, and delightful to behold, and she took the
fruit thereof."[323]

---

[320] Genesis 3:1-7
[321] See Genesis 2:15
[322] Song of Solomon 4:12
[323] Genesis 3:6

By doing nothing, Adam allowed the serpent to have his way with Eve, thus participating in exposing her to shame. To choose not to decide is to choose to neglect, and neglect is the grave sin of omission. After this tragic fall to the tempter, Adam and Eve "perceived themselves to be naked, they sewed together fig leaves, and made themselves aprons...and hid themselves from the face of the Lord God."[324] Shame always causes man to hide from goodness.

The consequences of human beings determining what is good and what is evil are devastating. Man often become bound by lust, resorting to objectifying the woman, repeatedly exposing her to his shame. Woman often resorts to the use of manipulation as a means to obtain affirmation and gratification.

Both Jacob and Joseph, in their abandonment to God's will, retreated from these disordered tendencies. As we will learn, Jacob retreated into the darkness of the night, crossing the ford of Jabbok, separating himself from family and possessions; but most importantly, separating himself from the ways of manipulation that were passed on to him by his mother. No longer would he be named Jacob, that is "usurper", or manipulator, but rather Israel.

Joseph, like Jacob, retreated into the silence, into the dark of night, apart from Mary, apart from his kin, to wrestle with God, to obtain wisdom as to how he should respond to his betrothed's pregnancy. Fearful of exposing Mary to his shame, Joseph would no longer be one who was known for fleeing from woman, but rather heralded as the protector—"Joseph most Chaste."

From Jacob and Joseph we learn that the *first step* to understanding and accepting God's will is to retreat into the darkness of silence, away from the world and its ever-multiplying distractions. As mentioned in the Prayer of Faith, silence and entering the silence with the intention of listening to God is the indispensible means to knowing God's will.

---

[324]   See Genesis 7-8

How often do fathers forget this truth! If you, my brother, desire to have the mind of God, you must enter the silence, particularly during life's most challenging moments.

When he became aware of Mary's astonishing pregnancy, Joseph was determined to submit to God by doing what he thought was God's will: resolving to send her away quietly. How difficult this must have been for Joseph!

It would be foolish for us to believe that Joseph was simply concerned with how he might rid himself of Mary, the scandal and the discomfort associated with such an unprecedented situation. If this was the case, then Joseph could hardly be described as a "just man," as the divinely inspired Scriptures attest. Rather, the just character of Joseph is exemplified in his willingness to release Mary, to protect her from begin exposed to the shame of men, while believing this to be the will of God. By choosing to release Mary, Joseph granted God authority over his life, hopes, and future.

Whereas Adam submitted to his own will in exposing Eve to the shame of her nakedness, Joseph submitted to the will of God, refusing to unveil the New Eve, Mary; he "defended" her "garden," upholding her dignity and person.

> We see that at the beginning of the New Testament, as at the beginning of the Old, there is a married couple. But whereas Adam and Eve were the source of evil which was unleashed on the world, Joseph and Mary are the summit from which holiness spreads over the earth. The Savior began the work of salvation by this virginal and holy union, wherein is manifested his all-powerful will to purify and sanctify the family-that sanctuary of love and cradle of life.[325]

---

[325]  Paul VI, Discourse to the "Equipes Notre-Dame" Movement (May 4, 1970)

Joseph's acceptance of God's will afforded him the power and humility to accept the Virgin, and thus embark upon the project of building the archetype of the domestic church, the "sanctuary of love."

Indeed, Joseph submitted to God, allowing God to decide what is good and what is evil, and by doing so, Joseph is glorified by the God Whom he has glorified. We too, my brother, by submitting ourselves to God will also be glorified by glorifying God.

# DAY 66

## RECONCILIATION WITH GOD

### *Jacob's Reconciliation with Himself and With His God*

The same night he arose and took his two wives, his two maids, and his eleven children, and crossed the ford of the Jabbok. He took them and sent them across the stream, and likewise everything he had. And Jacob was left alone; and a man wrestled with him until the breaking of the day.[326]

Jacob had arrived at a crossroads in his tumultuous life. The fact that Jacob decided to send his wives, his maids, and all of his possessions ahead while remaining behind, alone in the darkness of the night, is highly significant. Removing himself from all of his family and possessions, while remaining behind in the night, is indicative of Jacob retreating, separating himself from the world, determined to seek the Lord in the spiritual darkness of his life. Jacob was not simply alone in the darkness of the night, but left alone in the darkness of his own solitude, recognizing that his life was not in his own hands, and his future was beyond any human strategy. Jacob realized that his life and future were in the hands of God, and therefore he remained behind, separating himself from the world, in order to seek God, and to obtain an answer to his prayer for help in the matter of his confrontation with Esau.

---

[326] Genesis 32: 22-24

It was in the darkness of night that a man came and "wrestled with Jacob until the breaking of day."[327] This encounter proves to be the decisive turning point in Jacob's life, a time of reconciliation with himself and reconciliation with his God. The entirety of Jacob's life that preceded this event—the multiplication of humiliations and trials which began with his act of duplicity in stealing the blessing from his father—was gathered into this climactic moment in which he wrestled with God, longing to receive God's blessing justly. Indeed, Jacob, though crushed beneath many humiliations, desired to move beyond his guile-filled past, and press on in fortitude to build a future for his family.

In other words, Jacob wrestled not against God, but wrestled with God against himself. This wrestling encounter was not only a collision between two men, but a collision between a man of the past, wounded and full of brokenness; and a man of the future; a new man full of promise. We must not believe, dear brother, that God submitted to Jacob, allowing him to somehow prevail over the power of the Almighty God. Rather we must believe that God empowered Jacob to prevail over his own past, to defeat himself, to repent of his guile, and submit to the Lord God of power and might.

When the man asked Jacob to release him, Jacob responded, "I will not let you go until you bless me."[328] Unwilling to relinquish his hold upon God, Jacob desperately clung to the mysterious man until he finally obtained the blessing rightly—a blessing given rather than a blessing stolen. We must not overlook the lessons contained within this account. God always desired to bless Jacob, and in fact did bless Jacob with the blessing of his fathers. Jacob wanted to know with absolute certainty that God had given him

---

[327]   Genesis 32:24

[328]   Genesis 32:26

the blessing. Yet the only way to have the peace of knowing he had God's blessing was by obtaining God's blessing in a just manner.

Rather than presenting himself as another and stealing the blessing from his blind father, Jacob presents himself, *just as he is*, face to face with the Living God, in order to receive the blessing in the fullness of light. The fact that Jacob wrestled throughout the night with the man until "the breaking of the day" indicates that Jacob fought through the darkness of his past, pressing himself upon God so that his sincerity might be seen by God in the fullness of light.

My brother, if we desire to receive not only the blessing of God, but the knowledge that we are blessed by God, we must present ourselves, just as we are, before God, to be known by God and to know God in the fullness of His light. To do so, we must present to the Lord our past with all of its mire and guilt along with our sincere desire to follow God. We must hold nothing back. By presenting all to God we will receive all from God.

> The man of God then said, "Let me go, for the day is breaking"
> But Jacob said, "I will not let you go unless you bless me." And he
> said to him, "What is your name?" And he said, "Jacob." Then he
> said, "Your name shall no more be called Jacob, but Israel, for you
> have striven with God and with men, and have prevailed"....And
> there he blessed him.[329]

From that decisive moment on Jacob was a new man: "Israel, one who has striven with God and men and prevailed."[330] Jacob became the victor only by admitting his original loss; only by reconciling with the God Whom he had offended with guile.

---

[329]   Genesis 32:26-29
[330]   Genesis 32:28

# DAY 67

## Joseph's Reconciliation with Himself and God

"But as he considered this . . ."[331]

As stated previously, this passage from Matthew (1:18-25) is loaded with rich spiritual insights, particularly pertinent to fatherhood. It is like a sculpture that can be viewed from multiple angles, and viewed by numerous admirers in many ways. By examining this scripture verse from different vantage points, we will be able to obtain a more complete picture of this work of art inspired by God.

We have already interpreted this scripture in light of St. Joseph's desire for greatness, his acceptance of humiliations, his obedience to God and the law, his great mercy toward his neighbor, and his exemplary faith; but now we will discuss how these same actions demonstrate Joseph's capacity to wrestle with God against himself.

Even after he had resolved to dismiss the Virgin, Joseph persevered in prayer, refusing to cease his considerations until he had arrived at the answer his informed conscience demanded. Wrestling with God, he laid siege to heaven, refusing to release his grip on God until God released Joseph from his perplexed conscience.

"As he considered this an angel appeared to him in a dream,"[332] and "when he woke he did as the angel of the Lord commanded him."[333] Though Joseph had decided to "send her (Mary) away

---

[331] Matthew 1:20
[332] Matthew 1:20
[333] Matthew 1:24

quietly," the burden of the circumstance weighed heavily upon his heart, causing him to ponder the matter even while sleeping.

What were Joseph's wrestlings? Who was Joseph wrestling with? Joseph contended with himself, his desires for personal greatness, his desire for happiness within marriage, his desire for Mary and his desire to follow God's law. Joseph "did not know how to deal with Mary's 'astonishing' motherhood. He certainly sought an answer to this unsettling question, but above all he sought a way out of what was for him a difficult situation."[334] Yet, rather than fleeing, Joseph remained alone, in a personal solitude before God, longing for God's plan to be revealed.

In the darkness of night, Joseph wrestled with his own fears and temptations to flee the situation. Joseph, however, remained before God, wrestling with God against his weakened self, determined to receive God's direction, and even His blessing.

As the evening of the spiritual tempest diminished, the dawn from on high shone upon Joseph, casting light upon the future direction demanded of him. Joseph refused to release the matter until God released Joseph. Joseph remained in the darkness of solitude until the light of God's direction shone in his heart: "Do not fear to take Mary your wife..."

By persevering in this manner, Joseph received the blessing of his fathers, in the blessing of the person of Mary and in the child that dwelled within her, and thus, Joseph reconciled himself with his true calling and his God. By virtue of Christ in Mary, Joseph had become a father of many nations; a father of descendents more numerous than the stars.

---

334   Pope John Paul II, *Redemptoris Custos,* 3

# DAY 68

### Jacob's Fortitude

Jacob's perseverance allowed him to conquer and subdue himself, thus being liberated from his past of beguiling and grasping; only then was he able to receive the blessing of reconciliation from God. Within you also, my dear brother, exists a terrible battle between your fears and the longing for conquest, especially the conquest of your disordered self. If you desire to become a true man, aspire to the challenge of conquering something apparently greater than yourself: your fears, your doubts, and your past. Beware, my brother, for fear, if not properly transformed into trust, will become a power greater than yourself, evolving into an alter ego which will subdue your interior being, crushing your desire to become a valiant, holy defender of the domestic church, and instead deforming you into a coward who knows not the grace and power of the resurrected Christ.

As in the account of Jacob's wrestling with God, when we persevere in wrestling against our fears and against ourselves *with* God, the battle ends with the Son breaking into our darkness, scattering the ignorance of doubt, illuminating the rocky and narrow path that leads to building the domestic church.

## *Joseph's Prayerful Fortitude*

As with Jacob, Joseph, did not wrestle against God but with God against himself, his fears, his anxieties, his weaknesses, clinging to his Lord with the confidence that the blessing would be granted.

Joseph refused to control matters himself, but rather relied upon God to grant the solution. Joseph waited upon God for the answer, and by waiting he allowed God to purify his soul. Submitting to this process of purification, Joseph became entirely receptive to the divine plan, reconciling himself with his littleness—an act which in the end made him great.

As he actively rested in prayer, Joseph's desire for greatness became authentic. When the greatness Joseph desired appeared to be diminishing, Joseph chose to cling to the end rather than the means to the end, to the Creator rather than the creature, to God rather than his wife. There is a fine line between passively avoiding action and actively waiting. Prayer removes obstacles though the person praying appears not to be moving. Prayer is active though the man praying appears to be passive. Through prayer, a man who appears passive can actually wrestle with God against his fears, and by the grace of God, prevail.

Dear brother, in the person of Joseph there is reconciliation between fallen man, plagued by a desire for greatness, and the chosen servant who desired to become great by giving the Great One glory. Within Joseph lived the man who inherited concupiscence and the inability to love woman perfectly, but also the chosen servant who, redeemed by God's grace, persevered in upholding woman's dignity at the expense of self. With the angelic salutation, God offered Joseph the grace of redemption, granting him the fortitude to become a man who loved woman rightly.

*Establishing the Domestic Church*

# DAY 69

## ESTABLISHING THE DOMESTIC CHURCH

Dear brother, keep in mind that these reflections on humility and fortitude are for the purpose of preparing you to build the domestic church: a home wherein you, as the spiritual leader of your family, will lead your family to union with God. Your family's holiness should continually be your primary focus and chief proximate end, second only to your own personal holiness and pursuit of God.

By leading your own family to holiness, you will also achieve holiness, for in helping you fulfill your vocation to lead your family to God, God will be leading you to Himself.

We must not overlook this point. Many fathers, in pursuit of their own personal sanctification, neglect their vocational duties, choosing an idealistic personification of their personal sainthood and thus miss the mark of sanctification altogether. The true father discovers *within the mines of his fatherly vocation* the gems of inspiration to raise his children to holiness, and in doing so, discovers his own need for holiness. A father's desire for his child's holiness spurs him on to holiness; a father's desire for his child to reconcile with his brothers encourages a father to be reconciled with others. How could a father expect his child to perform an action from his heart that his father does not perform from his heart?

Every good father is determined to provide a house for his family to live in, but he must be even more determined to provide a house of worship for his God. The house of worship is not built by a father alone but by God, lest the father labor in vain.

The Three Components of Building the Domestic Church

As stated previously, from Jacob and Joseph we will learn the elements needed to succeed in building the domestic church. First, a father must reconcile himself to his brother; second, a father must detach himself from the worldly past; third, he must receive the Mother of God as his own, and by receiving her, receive the Son, Who is his family's ladder to heaven.

# DAY 70

Being reconciled to one's brothers is an ongoing action, yet those large unsettled enmities between you and your fellow man must be reconciled if your children are to learn how to "be perfect as the heavenly Father is perfect." By loving "those who persecute you," and "forgiving your enemies," you become an example of God's perfection living in the midst of a sinful world, while also transmitting the promise of a freedom grounded in purity of heart to your own children.

One of the greatest enemies to successfully building the domestic church is a hypocritical heart, by which you demand forgiveness from your children and yet have not forgiven your own enemies. Eventually, your children will discover your own hypocrisy and believe your faith to be a deception, possibly believing the Christian faith a fraud altogether. Loving your enemies by forgiving them is foundational to transmitting the purity of heart, demanded by Christ, to your children.

Reconciling with our enemies, or with those who have injured us, will serve as a continual test of our souls, indicating whether or not we are allowing ourselves to be open to the guidance of the Holy Spirit, Who will animate us to erect the domestic church.

In fact, reconciling with one's enemies, or with those who live in opposition to our beliefs, is a continual transitional stage between wrestling with God and building the domestic church When we strive to reconcile with those who have injured us, we wrestle with God against ourselves, against our pride and our desire to remain resentful. In this striving against our resentful pride we have the opportunity to overcome the old man so laden with sin, and by the power of Christ's redemptive grace, to experience the freedom to love our enemies and pass on such love to our family.

This striving with and overcoming of resentfulness towards one's neighbor is fundamental for a father who desires holiness within his home. Indeed, this is one reason that "forgive us our sins, as we forgive those who trespass against us," is one of the petitions of the Our Father. To cry out, "forgive us," is fundamental to our relationship with others and with God, and should be a central concern for fathers, for it is the essence of fatherhood. Indeed, if we desire to be perfect as our heavenly Father is perfect, we must learn to forgive just as He forgives. "Forgive one another as the Heavenly Father has forgiven you."[335]

This is a commandment given to all, but has a certain resonance with fathers, for if a father desires to be an image of the Heavenly Father he must strive to forgive as his Father in heaven has forgiven him.

Without reconciling ourselves with our brother, in vain do we endeavor to build the domestic church. For why should God be merciful, helping us build a temple in His name, if we are not merciful toward the temple of the Holy Spirit which is our brother?

It is never enough to reconcile ourselves only with God, just as it is never enough to reconcile ourselves only with man. We must reconcile ourselves to God Who reconciled man to Himself, and by doing so we will reconcile ourselves to man, who upon receiving our reconciliation may be inspired to reconcile himself to God. God grants us the strength necessary to reconcile with our brother, thus strengthening our brother to be fully reconciled to God. If you, my fellow father, are aspiring to reconcile your family to God, you

---

[335]   See Ephesians 4:32

must first be an example to your family of one who has reconciled himself with the family of God.

To build a temple, a domestic church wherein the Holy Presence of God dwells, a father must be a minister of reconciliation, becoming a peacemaker whose example leads his family to holiness. Throughout your many years of fatherhood, you will most certainly wrestle with God. There will be times when the brother to whom you must reconcile yourself is your wife or your child. Family life, as beautiful and glorious as it may be, will have moments of tension and interpersonal difficulties. Yet we must be quick to reconcile with one another, "forgiving one another just as Christ has forgiven" us.[336] Be reconciled to them, for this act is one of the great foundation stones upon which the domestic church is built.

Some will say that we must reconcile ourselves with our brother before reconciling with God, for Christ said, "If you are offering your gift at the altar, and remember that your brother has something against you, leave your gift there before the altar and go; first be reconciled to your brother, and then come and offer your gift."[337] Our Lord says that we should first be reconciled to our brother before offering worship; yet man cannot, of his own ability, be reconciled to His brother from his heart without the grace of God. Therefore he must reconcile himself with the truth that God grants us the grace and humility to reconcile with our brother. By reconciling with this truth, a man begins to reconcile himself to the ways of God and receives the grace to be reconciled to his brother, thus making his act of worship a complete act of reconciliation.

---

[336]  ibid

[337]  Matthew 5:23-24

# DAY 71

## Jacob's Reconciliation with His Brother

"The sun rose upon him as he passed Penuel, limping because of his thigh,"[338] for when the mysterious figure who wrestled with Jacob "saw that he did not prevail against Jacob, he touched the hollow of this thigh; and Jacob's thigh was put out of joint."[339] Indeed, the limp that would plague Jacob for the remainder of his life served as a perpetual reminder of his true identity: a man who is weak in himself, and yet made strong by God.

As the sun cast its early morning rays upon Jacob, a new knowledge of himself as Israel shone in his heart. Though physically weakened due to his disjointed thigh, Jacob was strengthened in spirit to meet his nemesis.

> And Jacob lifted up his eyes and looked, and behold, Esau was coming, and four hundred men with him. So he divided the children among Leah and Rachel and the two maids. And he put the maids with their children in front, then Leah with her children, and Rachel and Joseph last of all. *He himself went on before them,* bowing himself to the ground seven times, until he came near to his brother.[340]

---

[338] Genesis 32:31

[339] Genesis 32:25

[340] Genesis 33: 1-3 emphasis added

My brother, notice how Jacob, as the new man Israel, encounters his brother with whom he was formerly at enmity. Jacob was
indeed a new man, for he went before all of his family, leading
the way to their undetermined destiny. This was a man who had
humbled himself and learned the art of fortitude imbued with self
sacrifice. Jacob was willing to protect his family and to be the first
to meet his former adversary. Like Christ Who, at the end of His
short life, arose in prayer and went before his disciples to be the
first to meet his betrayer, Jacob arose and desired to be the first to
meet his enemy. Like Christ, Who fell prostrate upon the ground
and prayed, "Father, not my will but thine be done," Jacob bowed
before not only Esau, but God in the number of perfection—that
is, seven times—as a symbol of his perfect repentance and submission to the holy will of God. Jacob united the humble invitation to
reconciliation with his brother with his worship of the God Who
could deliver him from his dire situation.

"But Esau ran to meet him, and embraced him, and fell on his
neck, and kissed him, and they wept." Jacob's sincere act of reconciliation was received by Esau in a profoundly moving manner. Notice,
my brother, that in the act of reconciliation Jacob did not make
excuses, nor did he attempt to justify himself, but rather "counted
the other better than himself."[341]

When "Esau raised his eyes and saw the women and the children and said, 'Who are these with you?' Jacob said 'The children
whom God has graciously given your servant.'" [342] By referring to
himself as Esau's servant, Jacob demonstrated his profound humility. Yet Jacob not only revealed his own identity in relationship to
Esau but also, in all humility, revealed Esau's identity in relationship
to himself when he responded to Esau's question, "What do you
mean by all this company which I am met?", by saying, "To find

---

[341]   See Philippians 2:3

[342]   Genesis 33:5

favor in the sight of my lord." Jacob three times more referred to Esau as his lord.

Learn from Jacob, who demonstrated that reconciliation with one's brother demands that we identify ourselves as his servant and him as our lord, and by doing so experience the freedom for which Christ has set us free. In this we fulfill St. Peter's command: "therefore be imitators of Christ,"[343] Who Himself said, "I did not come to be served but to serve and lay my life down as a ransom for many."[344] Indeed, by understanding ourselves as the servant and our brother as our lord we lay down our life as a ransom for our family. When a child sees his father sacrifice his pride, the child will more likely be inspired to become a follower of Christ, knowing that there exists no earthly power that allows man to perform such an action.

---

[343] See Ephesians 5:1
[344] See Matthew 20:28

# DAY 72

## Joseph's Reconciliation with Mary

The strength of a man lies not in his physical grandeur or ability to impress with bodily power and might, but rather in his humble character. God's "pleasure is not in the strength of the horse, nor his delight in the legs of a man; the LORD delights in those who fear him, who put their hope in his unfailing love."[345]

Joseph's response to the crisis of Mary being pregnant without his cooperation could be misinterpreted as weakness: he fled. Joseph fled from the temptation to expose Mary to shame, and by dismissing her—though he believed his actions to be just—he actually risked dismissing himself from his God-given call to greatness. But what was Joseph really fleeing from?

Joseph's decision to leave Mary could have been interpreted by both the villagers of Nazareth and family members as an act of abandonment. His betrothed's pregnancy is discovered and he leaves. Such a perception of Joseph's action would have certainly exposed Mary to significant shame. Joseph, despite his unwillingness to expose Mary publicly, would not have been present to defend Mary and protect her from the insinuations, suspicions and accusations of the locals in response to the highly scandalous situation. How can Joseph's act of fleeing be reconciled with the truth that he was "unwilling to expose Mary to shame?" Joseph, by leaving, would have shielded Mary from shame—but not completely.

---

[345] Psalm 147:10-11

As stated previously, we can only interpret Joseph's unwillingness to expose Mary to shame as his own resolve to avoid and resist
exposing her to his fallen nature. Joseph did not suspect Mary of
infidelity, and therefore the shame from which he desired to protect her from was his concupiscence. Joseph fled from the temptation to shadow Mary under the cloak of his fallen nature. This is
important with regards to the humble character needed of a man
who desires to build the domestic church. Within the drama of
Joseph's act of fleeing we discover a timeless wisdom that describes
the type of person and character God elects to use in establishing
the Kingdom of God.

Moses, when called by God to go to Pharaoh and demand the
release of Israel, sensed his unworthiness and lack of ability, and yet
God selected him to carry out His plan. What Moses believed to be
a deficiency in himself was precisely the character through which
God manifested His strength and power.

Joseph did not believe himself to be worthy of the Virgin,
who was full of the divine presence, and therefore he resolved
to not expose her to his weakness and deficiency. Like Moses, it
was Joseph's humble character that caused him to believe himself
unworthy of the call to greatness. Yet, the humility that drove
Joseph from Mary was the very character that God used to manifest his glory.

Joseph believed himself to be unworthy of Mary's purity and
profound holiness, and because of his humility God called him to
return to her and uphold her dignity. Joseph did not believe himself to have the level of chastity needed to love the Virgin rightly,
and because of this humility God sent Joseph to Mary to become
"Joseph most Chaste." Precisely in the area that Joseph believed
himself to be weak God manifested His strength. Indeed, as with
Jacob's limp, Joseph's celibacy served as a perpetual reminder of his
human weakness while also reminding him of the divine strength

imparted to him. Joseph's reconciliation with Mary became Joseph's reconciliation with his call for greatness.

My fellow father, many men, in the context of their vocation of fatherhood and marriage, believe themselves to be unworthy, lacking the interior strength and resolve to be a great husband and father. It is precisely through this sense of weakness that God will manifest his strength, empowering you to become who you are called to be: a father on earth like the Father in heaven.

Many men, however, use their weakness as an excuse to indulge in sin. For example, a man may believe himself to be weak in the area of chastity, and rather than submitting his weakness to God and undergoing the process of redemption, he surrenders to Satan, believing that indulging in lust will grant him masculine strength. Man's strength, un-submitted to God, often subjects him to weakness, whereas man's weakness submitted to God makes him strong.

If you, my brother, are obedient to God's call, you will encounter many trials. These tests will bring you face to face with your weaknesses and strengths. Many men, during such trials, while experiencing the reality of their weakness, flee from their post to defend their wives, leaving not only their wives, but also their children inescapably vulnerable to the ways of evil.

Joseph's reconciliation with Mary stands as an example worthy of imitating. My brother, reconciliation with your brother may often mean that you reconcile with your "sister, bride."[346] Often, only after a man has been married does he discover the depth of his personal deficiencies and weaknesses in the area of how he relates to women. Rather than fleeing from this weakness, you, my brother, like Joseph, will benefit from surrendering these deficiencies to the Lord and allowing Him to supply the strength needed to reconcile with your wife.

---

[346]  See Song of Songs 4:9

# DAY 73

## BUILDING THE DOMESTIC CHURCH: DETACHMENT

Many men have embarked upon the endeavor to build a house from the ground up. Yet many of these men, having a great number of possessions, have built their future home contingent upon their past. They have chosen to build a new future by building a new space that is dependent upon fitting within it the possessions they have accumulated throughout their lives. In this way, a man does not build a new future, but rather builds a future around and upon his past.

My brother, God will call you to detach yourself from some aspects of your past in order to allow you to successfully erect the domestic church. Indeed, He may call you to move to new lands, sever precious relationships, or sell possessions in an effort to free you from impeding encumbrances that have the potential of diminishing your power to build an environment that fosters the growth of a holy family.

Our Lord calls us to give up lands, fathers, mothers, brothers and sisters for the sake of Him and His Kingdom. Indeed, when building the domestic church, even our closest relatives, our career or our friends can all prove to be harmful influences that diminish or mitigate our power to fulfill our God-ordained mission. You must be determined to remove these hindrances from your vocational path. If you do not exercise this fatherly right, your charitable authority will be compromised, having minimal effect upon your family.

Indeed, the Lord arranged marital life so that "a man leaves his father and mother and clings to his wife."[347] A man is called by God to detach himself, at some level, from his past in order to build his future.

Let us turn to Jacob and Joseph and discover how God called each of them to remove certain aspects of their pasts to make room so that the presence of God could live among their families. Indeed, from these two, we will discover that detachment from these hindrances is essential to the successful building of the domestic church.

---

[347]  See Genesis 2:24

# DAY 74

## Jacob's Detachment: Casting off Idols

After the beautiful event of Jacob's reconciliation with his elder brother, Jacob "journeyed to Succoth and built for himself a house."[348] After twenty years of exile, Jacob's dream of building a house for his family was finally becoming a reality. Jacob's quest and desire for greatness was inherently linked to the desire of building a house, a physical domain for his family. This seemed to be Jacob's dream, "to settle down" with his family; to provide a safe, stable, familial environment. Yet, as we will see, this is only a fragment, a symbol, if not a shadow of the true goal. The physical domain, though visible, is minimal in comparison to the spiritual domain, which God calls every father to build in His name.

> Jacob came safely to the city of Shechem, which is in the land of Canaan, on his way from Paddanaram; and he camped before the city. And from the sons of Hamor, Shechem's father, he bought for a hundred pieces of money the piece of land on which he had pitched his tent. There he erected an altar and called it El-Elohe-Israel, (The God, the God of Israel).[349]

After Jacob's lengthy exile, after exposing woman to his shame, growing his family, reconciling with God, with himself, and with his brother, Jacob was led full-circle to the land of his fathers, where

---

[348] Genesis 33:17

[349] Genesis 33:18-20

he finally erected a house. Jacob's intentions had the character of nobility, for he not only purchased land for his family and cattle, but also erected an altar dedicated to the Lord. Indeed, Jacob's motivations to establish a home and establish a place of worship were pure.

Yet, after Jacob had completed these noble acts, God called Jacob to "go to Bethel and dwell there; and make there an altar to the God Who appeared to you when you fled from your brother Esau."[350]

Why would God summon Jacob and his family to return to Bethel? What difference is there between an altar built in Shechem and an altar previously built in Bethel?

It seems that God expected more from Jacob and more from Jacob's family. Peering ahead into the text, we discover that Jacob's family was not entirely the Lord's, for they were attached to the idols of foreign gods, and Jacob was aware of this.

> So Jacob said to his household and to all who were with him, "Put away the foreign gods that are among you, and purify yourselves, and change your garments; then let us arise and go up to Bethel, that I may make there an altar to the God Who answered me in the day of my distress and has been with me wherever I have gone."

Jacob purchased land, made booths for his cattle, pitched his tent and even built an altar to the God of Israel in the land of Shechem, while knowing that his family had become attached to foreign gods. By calling Jacob to return to Bethel, God was reminding Jacob that He is the God Who provided for him in his exile, while also awakening in him the understanding of what is demanded of the father of a family.

---

[350]   Genesis 35:1

By calling Jacob to return to the holy place of Bethel, God was making Jacob aware of his responsibility to lead his family to holiness by consecrating them to God. Indeed, the divine call for Jacob to return to Bethel inspired Jacob to command his family to return to God by detaching himself and his family from the vestiges of the past. Indeed, Jacob was called by God to break free from spiritual slavery to Laban and his house by casting off Laban's idols.

My brother, how rich is the significance and meaning behind these events. Jacob planned to build a house, a physical domain, for himself and his family, choosing the place and the manner that he would build it, attempting to dedicate his new domain to the Lord, while not requiring single-hearted worship from his family.

God, however, was teaching Jacob that a house built well must be a house built exclusively for God, with God, and by God; and that it must become a dwelling place not only for man and his family, but for God amidst the family. God was teaching Jacob that his house should be a sanctuary of worship wherein an altar is erected to provide a place for his entire family to worship and sacrifice to the Living God.

Jacob had built a house for the residence of men, but God, not satisfied, called him to build a house where God would dwell. Jacob sacrificed to build a house, but God commanded him to build a house for sacrifice.

It is also important to note that Bethel was south of Shechem, and yet God called Jacob, to "arise and go up to Bethel." In these words we discover that to build a house for God is to "go up," even if the direction is south. To build a house exclusively to the Lord, a house without idols, is to assist the family in their ascent toward union with God.

Dear brother, God does not desire to provide a house for your family to dwell in as much as He desires to provide a house where He will dwell with your family. Our Lord does not desire so much that a temple be built around you, but rather He desires that the temple be built within you and within your family.[351] This, my brother, is the purpose of the house: to provide a place wherein the domestic sanctuary can be built. Some adorn their homes with fine furniture and delightful décor, but we are called to decorate our domestic churches with the sapphires and emeralds of the gifts of the Holy Spirit, and to build her walls with the precious stones of the virtues.

---

[351]    See 1 Corinthians 3:16 and Tobit 13:10

# DAY 75

The holy pilgrimage to Bethel began with the father, Jacob, commanding his family to repent of their idol worship, to admit that the walls of their hearts had been breached by sin, to confess and offer the sacrifice of a contrite heart and be clothed anew by redemptive grace. These stages of repentance, commanded by Jacob, correlate directly with Psalm 51, the great repentant Psalm of David.

The first stage of true repentance consists of a confession that man's heart has been breached and overtaken by foreign gods, invaded by sin, and that his temple has become the dwelling place of demons rather than God. Man answers the command to put away all foreign gods with the response, "Have mercy on me O God...and blot out my transgressions, cleanse me from my sin! For I know my transgressions and my sin is ever before me."[352]

The Second stage is the purification of self, as Jacob commanded, "purify yourselves and change your garments." Obviously man cannot purify himself and wash away his own sins, for if this is a possibility then the death of Christ is void of meaning. This purification of self is the sacrifice of a contrite heart, where the sinner beseeches God to rebuild the walls of his heart, strengthening the bars of his gates that his soul may be protected by the God Who makes His dwelling therein. This purification is summed up in the words of the psalmist, "Purge me with hyssop and I shall be clean;

---

[352] Psalm 51

create in me a clean heart, O God, and put a new and steadfast spirit within me. Cast me not away from Thy Presence, and take not Thy Holy Spirit from me."³⁵³ By offering this heartfelt prayer of sacrifice, the sinner purifies himself by allowing the merciful God to purify him.

The third stage of repentance is the offering of lawful sacrifice upon the altar of God in God's house: "Let us arise and go up to Bethel, that I may make there an altar to the God Who answered me in the day of my distress." What is this lawful sacrifice that is needed after the sacrifice of a contrite heart is given? The psalmist explains:

> For Thou hast no delight in sacrifice; were I to give a burnt offer-
> ing, Thou wouldst not be pleased. The sacrifice acceptable to God
> is a broken spirit; a broken and contrite heart, O God, Thou wilt
> not despise.³⁵⁴

The sacrifice of a contrite heart is enough. However, the psalm continues,

> In thy good pleasure rebuild the walls of Jerusalem, then Thou
> wilt delight in right sacrifices.³⁵⁵

After the breached and crumbled walls of the sinner's heart have been restored by redemptive grace, God requests that the lawful sacrifice be made. Once the sinner has repented and confessed his sin, he is now asked to make the sacrifice that God desires, the Eucharistic sacrifice, which is the sacrifice of thanksgiving. We will discuss this in more detail in the Prayer of Meditation, but

---

[353]   ibid

[354]   ibid

[355]   ibid

for now it suffices to state that upon receiving absolution, we have been clothed anew in grace and are capable of offering the lawful sacrifice of the only One Who fulfilled the law perfectly, and Who offers Himself to the Father on behalf of the world. As we will see, The Eucharistic sacrifice is indeed a sacrifice of thanksgiving, wherein we thank the merciful God Who "Restores the joy of our salvation."[356]

For many, the walls of the family temple have been breached and the inner courts trampled by the invasion of sin and the attachment to false gods. Like Jacob, many fathers have mistakenly pursued their own path of holiness while neglecting to make the same demands upon their family, or have made no demands upon themselves or their family.

God, however, calls each father to return to Bethel, to His House, where not only the human father's temple, but those of his family, will be restored. God calls every father to Bethel to become reconciled with Him, to offer the sacrifice of a contrite heart which He will not spurn,[357] and in His goodness He will show favor to us and rebuild our walls of defense,[358] protecting us from further invasions of sin. Then He will strengthen the bars of our gates,[359] allowing us to please Him with lawful sacrifice, holocausts offered on His altar.[360]

My brother, understand how the domestic church is built! The Heavenly Father calls the earthly father to reconciliation, strengthening him, asking him to be united in faith with his wife so that his wife may be united in faith to God, so that together they may place the joyful burden of the faith upon their own children. By jointly worshipping, the married couple with their children will be

---

[356]   ibid

[357]   ibid

[358]   Reference to Psalm 51

[359]   Reference to Psalm 147

[360]   Reference to Psalm 51

allowing God to rebuild their temple, and thus ensuring that the Presence of God will dwell within them, undisturbed by the malicious threats of satanic invasions.

After beginning the process of rebuilding the temple of the earthly father, God calls the father to correspond to grace by participating in the project of building the domestic sanctuary. The father who has been taught by God to offer the sacrifice of a contrite heart in turn teaches his family to offer their contrite hearts in sacrifice as well. Every father is called to lead his family to reconciliation with God.

Jacob's family responded to his command and "gave to Jacob all the foreign gods that they had," "and he hid them under the tree near Shechem,"[361] a symbol of the cross of Christ where all men lay aside their idols. See, my brother, the confidence with which Jacob commanded his family to give up their gods and be reconciled to the true God. Jacob was able to command and lead his family to reconciliation with God only because he had been first reconciled with God. My brother, if you expect your family to be reconciled with God, you must also expect the same of yourself, living the example you desire for them to follow.

Do not recoil from your duty to command your family to give up all foreign gods, but also be careful not to command them to do what you have not already done, for this is hypocrisy. If you lay your idols at the foot of Christ's cross, your family will be able to do the same, and together your family may proceed to God's house to offer themselves in union with the lawful sacrifice of the Bread of Life. In this way, you have begun the project of building the domestic church.

---

[361]  Genesis 35:4

# DAY 76

JOSEPH'S DETACHMENT FROM THE PAST:
BUILDING A FUTURE

Like Jacob, who after fleeing Laban, had established a home in Shechem, but was called by God to move to Bethel, Joseph was called to leave the humble confines of Nazareth, Mary's family and his, their home, and trek to Bethlehem to be counted in the census.

God had called Jacob and his family to Bethel where they had cast off their idols to detach themselves definitively from the past and from Laban's influence. It was in Bethel, for the first time, that Jacob erected "a house for God."

In a similar manner, Mary and Joseph were called to journey to Bethlehem and not return to Nazareth for years. Indeed, God was calling Mary and Joseph to detach themselves from home, family, communal life, and their childhood past so that He might build them into *His* family: a family removed from impeding outside influences. Indeed, "every one that hath left house, or brethren, or sisters, or father, or mother, or wife, or children, or lands for my name's sake, shall receive an hundredfold, and shall possess life everlasting."[362] Mary and Joseph, in a real and painful way, detached themselves from all of this precisely *for* Jesus.

Initially, it appears that Mary and Joseph were only, for the short term, leaving Nazareth with hopes to lodge temporarily with Joseph's relatives in the small village of Bethlehem with the purpose

---

[362] Matthew 19:29

of being numbered in the census. Joseph, being a son of David, and being of the family of Bethlehem, certainly had some hope of being received by his kinsfolk.

It may be beneficial to our personal pursuit of erecting the domestic church to appreciate the level of detachment that God was demanding of Joseph. As mentioned in the "Prayer of Faith," obedience is the trailhead of personal triumphs in the pursuit of personal holiness. Obedience, however, also leads a man into various trials that test his personal character.

Triumph is only obtained through trial. Trials and tests are an essential factor in the making of a man of God. Examine the lives of the great saints, the men who, to this day, the Church honors and lauds. By studying their lives we discover that each of their heroic lives were plagued with trials and tests; tests which they passed. Obedience is a man's humble submission to God's invitation to enter the trial, the battle, to step more fully into the adventure of fatherhood.

Joseph faithfully submitted, time and time again, to the test, though at times reluctantly. By reflecting upon what Sacred Tradition refers to as the Joyful Mysteries, of which St. Joseph was a key player, we recognize that each of these crucial moments in salvation history are marked by intense challenges, struggles and trials in Joseph's life. Precisely because of the challenging quality of the test, with the passing of the test, the joy obtained is all the more intense.

By choosing Mary as his bride, Joseph entered the test of receiving his vocation by embracing the Virgin pregnant with child. Joseph initially hesitated, but ultimately submitted to the test. Joseph obeyed the laws of the Mosaic covenant, accepting his fatherly authority over the Christ child by naming Him and having the babe circumcised. Again, Joseph obeys. Later Joseph presents the Child to God, and yet in doing so he receives the prophetic words of Simeon, foretelling of Mary's broken heart. Joseph also submitted to yet another trial: he obeyed the command to be counted in Caesar's census. We must not overlook the quality of Joseph's obedience within this context. Perhaps the words of St. Paul describing submission to authorities will help us understand the depth of Joseph's act of obedience.

> Let everyone be subject to he higher authorities, for there exists no authority except from God, and those who exist have been appointed by God. Therefore he who resists the authority resists the ordinance of God; and they that resist bring on themselves condemnation. [363]

This understanding of secular authority proposed by St. Paul is a radical concept and can be particularly scandalous to those whose peoples and lands have been subdued by tyrannical and corrupt authorities. One cannot help but to consider those subjected to the authority of Hitler, Stalin, Napoleon, or Herod. Caesar's census could easily have been interpreted by a faithful Jew as an initiative to further subdue and control God's chosen people. By obtaining the name of a Jew, and numbering him among the subjects of the Roman empire, Caesar was, in a sense, proclaiming, "I own you," and "you are counted only as subjects to my authority." A zealous Jew may have believed that rebellion against such pagan tyranny was justified in the sight of God. Yet, Joseph obeyed the command.

---

[363]   Romans 13:1-3

# DAY 77

And all were going, each to his own town, to register. And Joseph
also went from Galilee out of the town of Nazareth into Judea to
the town of David, which is called Bethlehem - because he was of
the house and family of David - to register, together with Mary
his espoused wife, who was with child.[364]

Joseph, consequently, enters yet another unforeseen trial, another
hardship veiled by the future's shadow. Joseph, son of David,
returned to the city of the King, rich with his family's heritage,
to his kinsfolk, with the hopes of being welcomed. Mary, his
wife, was in the last stages of pregnancy and could deliver at any
moment. A seventy mile trek from Nazareth to Jerusalem upon a
donkey would have certainly assisted in inducing her into labor.
The circumstances are not wanting for the elements of an intense
trial. Indeed, there existed ample excuse for Joseph to dismiss
himself from obeying Caesar's decree to be numbered in his
worldwide census. And yet, Joseph obeyed God and submitted to
the trial, a situation that greatly tested Joseph's character.

Joseph, son of David, returned to "his own town," to his own "home" and
yet, here in his native village, among his kinsfolk,

---

[364] Luke 2:3-5

the days for [Mary] to be delivered were fulfilled. And she brought
forth her firstborn son, and wrapped him in swaddling clothes,
and laid him in a manger, because there was no room for them in
the inn.[365]

It was here, among his own kinsfolk, that Joseph encountered
the humiliation of being rejected: of not being able to find—or not
being offered—a home for Mary to deliver her child. One cannot
help but to surmise that news of Mary's pregnancy and its so-called
questionable character had reached Bethlehem.

Bethlehem, being a small village, and, at that time, of little
commercial status, was unlikely to have an "inn" existing in its
locale. The Greek word, which has typically been translated as
"inn", is Kataluma, which can be translated as "a loosening down"
(kata, "down", luo, "to loose"), a place where travelers untied their
packages from their beasts, and removed their girdles and sandals,
whereas the word Pandocheion is translated as "inn."[366] This indicates that the homes of the citizens of Bethlehem were closed to
Joseph, the son of David, and his delivering wife. At some level,
Mary and Joseph were rejected, for "there was no room for them"
among any of the villager's homes, and so they were allotted space
among the animals and beasts in a manger. Joseph was called by
God to the city of the King so that the true King could be born in
this village. In the "town of bread," in a manger, which often was
located beneath the actual residential dwelling, in a cave-like space,
the Bread of Life was born.

It seems that our Lord desired to be born among the low-
est, even lower than the lowliest villagers in Bethlehem, in order
to lift all to God above. Indeed, our Lord obeyed the census, to
be counted among the lowliest in order to count all as one with

---

[365]   Luke 2:6-7
[366]   See *Vines Greek New Testament Dictionary*

Himself, and because of this humility He is exalted above all in all whom He exalts.

Joseph accepted this rejection, this lowliness, this humiliation, and doing so, he received humility—Humility Himself—and the exalted glory of Christ. Such a rejection of a woman in her most vulnerable state, in her greatest moment of need, is a sore humiliation. Yet, Joseph set his face as flint, rising in fortitude, ensuring that the Virgin was provided a dwelling space for her to give birth to the Son of God. Indeed, in the lowly place, filled with the stench and baseness of beastly living, Joseph humbly prepared a suitable crib for the birth of the King of Heaven.

My brother, learn from Joseph that by detaching ourselves from creatures, from human beings, from material wants and comforts, we provide space for the Presence of God. Indeed, at the convergence of humiliations, if we embrace the virtue of humility and grow in fortitude we will be rewarded with the Presence of God. This was Joseph's reward. If we are to build the domestic church we must, like Jacob and Joseph, set our sights upon the one thing that make a house a home: the Presence of God living among the family.

My fellow father, obediently enter the trials set before you, detaching yourself from whatever hinders you from fulfilling the mission God has called you to embrace, and by doing so, you will "make a suitable place" for Jesus, the Son of God, to dwell among your family.

It is precisely in the context of being rejected and humiliated that Joseph prevailed, in detaching himself from outside worldly influences, fulfilling his vocational duty, proving himself to be a man of integrity, a husband of valor, who provided not only space for the Virgin birth, but ample space for God to dwell among his family.

# DAY 78

## THE ORIGINS OF THE DOMESTIC CHURCH

You, my brother, are called to greatness by means of the vocation of fatherhood, which lays upon you the demand to build the domestic church. To accomplish this task you will need a mother and a son. Every father is in need of the Mother, and every father must receive her Son as his own. Yes, my brother, you must receive the Mother to receive the Son, and you must receive the Son to be a father whose fatherhood reflects the Eternal Fatherhood of God to his own children and their mother. As we will see, only with the help of these two Persons does God promise true success to a father who desires to build the domestic church.

We have discussed the first two essential elements needed to erect the domestic church: to reconcile with our brothers and to cast off all idols. We will now discuss the other essential components needed to erect an environment which produces holy families: the House of God—the Mother of the Son—and the Ladder to Heaven—the Son of the Mother.

### Revisiting Bethel: Jacob's Ladder

It is important that we return to Jacob's first journey to Bethel in order to see how his second journey is typologically connected to Joseph.

Dear brother, let us return for a moment to Jacob's words, "Let us arise and go up to Bethel, that I may make there an altar to the

God who answered me in the day of my distress."[367] The day of Jacob's distress was the event of being driven into exile, in which he was forced to flee from the house of his father to protect his life from being slain by the vengeful Esau. After traveling, he came to a certain place, and taking one of the stones; he put it under his head and lay down to sleep.[368] "And he dreamed that there was a ladder set up on the earth, and the top reached to heaven; and behold, the angels of God were ascending and descending upon it! And behold the Lord stood above it."[369]

In his dream, God promised Jacob the land upon which he stood, descendents like the dust of the earth, the blessing of all the families of the earth through these descendants, and God's perpetual presence: "Behold I am with you and will keep you where ever you may go."[370]

Upon awakening, Jacob said, "Surely the Lord is in this place and I did not know it – how awesome is this place! This is none other than the house of God, and this is the gate of heaven."[371] He then took the stone which he slept on and poured oil over it calling the name of the place Bethel, that is House of God.[372]

It was only after many years of difficulty and trial that Jacob, heeding the command of God, decided to return to the "house of God" and sacrifice to his God. Taking his family to Bethel to offer this sacrifice, Jacob was proclaiming an oath to build the domestic church not as his own house, but as a house of God. It was during this return to Bethel that Jacob, as the new Israel, received from God the reiteration of the original blessing, and proclaimed with great confidence that the name of the place was Bethel.

---

[367]   Genesis 35:3
[368]   Genesis 28:11
[369]   Genesis 28:13
[370]   Genesis 28:15
[371]   Genesis 28:16-18
[372]   Genesis 28:18

God called Jacob to return to Bethel, to hearken back to the dream and the promise made to Jacob.

What do Jacob's return to Bethel and his encounter with God at Bethel indicate for us and our discussion of building the domestic church? Jacob's first encounter with God in the dream at Bethel is rich with significance, and will be of great assistance in helping us identify the essential elements needed to erect the domestic church. By comparing Jacob's dream to the dream of Joseph, wherein the angel of God spoke to this chaste spouse in regards to the Virgin, we will begin to understand the meaning of these elements. Indeed, Bethel, the stone, the dream, the ladder, the House of God, and the Gate of Heaven all have tremendous allegorical significance, which can be applied practically to our vocation as fathers.

# DAY 79

Joseph fled from the temptation to expose the woman Mary to shame, and by dismissing her, he sent himself into exile from his vocation, from his God-given call to greatness. It was in this exile of solitude that Joseph considered the matter of Mary's pregnancy. Sleeping upon the matter of the child in the virgin's womb, Who would become the "stone rejected by the builders,"[373] the "stone cut from a mountain by no human hand,"[374] which would break into pieces the earthy kingdoms, Joseph was given the grace to understand that the child was indeed of the Holy Spirit.

Like Jacob, Joseph wrestled with God against himself, and receiving the message that the dawn from on high had taken His abode in Mary, he awoke with the intent to reconcile himself to the Virgin. Awakening from the dream, Joseph returned to the Virgin, to the true and new Bethel, the "House of God,"[375] the place and the person where the Ladder, "God with us,"[376] was set upon the earth, taking His place among men.

Joseph's reconciliation with the Virgin was a proclamation that "Surely the Lord is in this place! How awesome is this place! This is none other than the Gate of Heaven!"

---

[373]  Psalm 118:22

[374]  Daniel 2:45

[375]  Litany of Loreto

[376]  Matthew 1:23

In his angelic dream, Joseph received the grace for the temple of God to be rebuilt within him,[377] enabling him to receive the temple of the new Bethel, the Virgin Mary. Receiving her, he received the foundational stone, Jesus, upon which he would build the domestic church.

My brother, from this typological comparison, we have been gifted with the knowledge that the pursuit of holiness for the family is most dependent upon the father receiving the Mother, and upon the father receiving the Son as the cornerstone of his domestic church. Indeed, "Joseph took Mary as his wife,"[378] that is, he took her into his home, and receiving the Mother he received the Son.

My brother, follow the example of Joseph, run to the Virgin Mary, to that new Bethel, the House of God; receive her as your own and love her, entrusting your life to her, sacrificing your life for the sake of her Son, Who sacrificed His life for your sake. For how can you love your own children's mother rightly if you cannot love the Son of God's Mother? How can you build a temple, a house for the Son, if you cannot receive the House of God He built for Himself?

Do not be fooled by those who say that Christ alone is needed. Did the Christ Who needs nothing not purposefully need the Virgin? He did need her and we need Him; and needing Him we need like Him, needing the Virgin. The Son acquired the flesh which redeemed the world from His own mother. The Son fully consecrated Himself to His mother by giving Himself completely to her in the act of the incarnation. Do we believe that we are somehow above Christ?

We must ask ourselves this question: Who was the first to entrust himself to Mary? The heavenly Father. He entrusted His Son and His Spirit completely to this beloved bride. My brother,

---

[377]   Reference Tobit 13:10
[378]   Matthew 1:24

our dignity and honor as fathers is to be an icon of the heavenly Father. If we are to be like the Father in heaven, we must entrust ourselves to the Blessed Virgin.

Indeed the first step Joseph took in receiving his vocation must also be our first step: we must receive Mary into our home, that is, into our very soul. This first step, however must not simply be a one-time action, but rather should become an ongoing commitment to entrusting our life to her.

The success of building your house for God depends upon your reception of the House of God. Invite this House into yours. Every father needs the Mother and every father needs the Son. How righteous it is to consecrate your fatherhood to the Mother to Whom the Son consecrated Himself! She is, as the Church proclaims in her litanies, "The House of God, The Gate of Heaven," the way to the Way, the gate to the Ladder Who is the Son of man, the Son of Joseph,[379] Whom "you will see the angels ascending and descending upon."[380]

---

[379] John 1:45
[380] John 1:51

# DAY 80

Joseph's embrace of the Mother and the Son gave reason and purpose for building the domestic church, and thus he fulfilled the promise given to Jacob concerning him: "and by your descendents shall all families on the earth bless themselves."[381] It is by virtue of the Holy Family that all families receive the blessing of God, and it is by virtue and example of Joseph's reception of the new Bethel and her Son that all fathers are blessed by God. The Holy Family contains within itself the three essential elements that comprise a holy family: first, a father who has reconciled his entire life to God by repenting and refusing to have any idols; second, the Blessed Mother; and third, the Son of God.

If you desire, my brother, for your family to be blessed like the Holy Family, it is imperative that you be a father who has reconciled his life to God, who has received both the Mother and the Son of God into his very own temple, dedicating himself to sacrifice for the two. For if you sacrifice yourself for the Mother and the Son, you are sacrificing yourself for your own children and their mother. Joseph is the exemplar who received the Son of God from the Mother of God, and if we desire to be the faithful father

---

[381] Genesis 28:14

that Joseph was, we must do what he did and receive the Son from the Mother. This Gate of Heaven is the House of God that contains the true Gate Who is the Ladder to heaven and is heaven itself. How mysterious this is! Yet the success of our fatherhood depends upon our acceptance of and belief in this mystery.

If we have the heart to accept this truth, we will become like Joseph, who beheld the unfolding of the mystery of redemption as he studied the living picture of the Madonna and Child. Respectfully watching the Virgin, studying her actions of tender love, Joseph was privileged to see the life of Christ through the eyes and the heart of the Virgin Mother, meditating upon these mysteries of the Rosary lived out in motion pictures. If we dare to be like Joseph, receiving the Virgin Mother, we too will be given the gift to view the mystery of redemption through the heart of Mary, a heart within which Mary kept hidden the mysteries of God.

This pierced heart is a storehouse of mystical treasures, opened for all who are willing to raise their cup and be filled from the over-flow and abundance of her wisdom and love. My brother, much like Joseph, you have access to drink from the treasures of the mysteries that flow from Mary's pierced heart. If you choose to lift your chalice to this pierced heart of the Virgin, you will advance quickly, reaching a far superior state of holiness than your own efforts alone could give. Just as the just Joseph received the reward of Christ's Presence into his family by receiving the Virgin, so too, by your reception of the Mother, the Presence of the Son will continually be with your family.

Let us then arise from our dream of building the domestic church and, like Joseph, set up the Stone of Christ as a pillar for our own families. By providing the true House of God—Jesus the Son—a house, Joseph was helping the Stone become the Eternal House of God Who gave all humanity divine residence. Persevere in prayer, my brother, and you will erect a home that is a true domestic church, a temple in which the Presence of God dwells with delight. The father who builds his house upon the Stone of Christ will one day awake from his dream to discover that his desire has been fulfilled.

The Prayer of Perseverance inspires a father to provide a temple that produces new temples of Christ, who assist in the transformation of the world. The project of building a temple that produces children who become temples of the Living God is amongst the greatest and most essential missions of mankind. This task is worthy of you and your desire to greatness; this vocation is your call to greatness.

Persevere then, pressing on, seeking God's guidance in life's litany of daily activities. Fear not that these duties are immersed in the regularity and often mundane character of life. As with prayer, when our duties become dry and common, you must dive deeper into this dryness, waiting for God to speak. If you persevere in this way, you will eventually receive divine insights that are akin to the heavenly dreams of Joseph and Jacob. Indeed, a father must persevere in prayer, believing in the promise given by God to Jacob at Bethel, "I will not leave you until I have done that of which I have spoken to you."[382] Yes, my brother, He will not abandon those who persevere in prayer until they have done His will.

---

[382]    Genesis 28:15

# COMING 2014

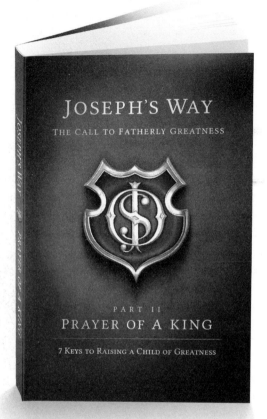

# JOSEPH'S WAY

## THE CALL TO FATHERLY GREATNESS

### VOLUME II

# PRAYER OF A KING

## 7 KEYS TO RAISING A CHILD OF GREATNESS

JosephsWayBook.com